Multilateral Aspects of the Disarmament Debate

Published for and on behalf of the United Nations

Taylor & Francis

New York • Philadelphia • Washington, D.C. • London

USA	Publishing Office:	Taylor & Francis New York Inc. 79 Madison Ave., New York, NY 10016-7892
	Sales Office:	Taylor & Francis Inc. 1900 Frost Road, Bristol, PA 19007
UK		Taylor & Francis Ltd. 4 John St., London WC1N 2ET

Multilateral Aspects of the Disarmament Debate

First published 1989
Printed in the United States of America

Library of Congress Cataloging in Publication Data

Multilateral aspects of the disarmament debate.

"Published for and on behalf of the United Nations."
Papers from two meetings of experts held by the United Nations Dept. for Disarmament Affairs.
1. Nuclear disarmament—Congresses. 2. Disarmament—Congresses I. United Nations. Dept. for Disarmament Affairs.
JX974.7.M85 1989   327.1'74   89-5090
ISBN 0-8448-1616-7

Contents

Introduction

The United Nations Department for Disarmament Affairs held two meetings of experts in Dagomys, USSR, entitled "After Reykjavik: Planning for the Nineties" and "Verification of Arms Limitation Agreements." The first meeting, 8–12 June 1987, focused on three major topics: conventional weapons (including regional agreements, reduction and elimination of conventional weapons, confidence-building measures, and verification); nuclear weapons (including reduction and elimination of nuclear weapons, cessation and banning of nuclear tests, establishment of nuclear weapon-free zones in various regions of the world, and prevention of nuclear war); and international security and outer space.

The second meeting, held 11–15 April 1988, examined the multilateral aspects of the verification of arms limitation and disarmament agreements. The 35 experts from more than 20 countries participating in the meeting discussed the conceptual issues and the technical aspects of verification.

Regarding conceptual aspects, the participants focused on issues such as an overview of the relationship between verification of arms control and disarmament agreements and security, principles of verification, lessons from existing arrangements, institutional aspects and the human factor, and openness, transparency, and confidence-building. The technical issues included topics such as multilateral aspects of the verification of underground nuclear explosions, scientific and technological progress in verification techniques, and whether there is a growing gap between advances in weapons systems and verification capabilities. The meeting also addressed verification issues relevant for the future.

Discussion at the meetings was based on presentations of the papers published here in chronological order. The lists of participants in both of these meetings are included. The meetings were financed entirely from the contribution of the Soviet Union to the United Nations Trust Fund for the World Disarmament Campaign.

Part One

"After Reykjavik: Planning for the Nineties"

**United Nations Meeting of Experts
Dagomys, USSR, 8–12 June 1987**

Chapter 1

Conventional Weapons

CONVENTIONAL ARMS CONTROL IN EUROPE: OBJECTIVES AND PROBLEMS

*Ludger Buerstedde**

Since the summit meeting in Reykjavik, it has become apparent that East-West relations in the security field have reached a watershed. The United States and the Soviet Union are preparing to place their strategic nuclear rivalry on a new footing. This also has consequences for the security situation in Europe. Under these circumstances, the Europeans must participate actively in the search for new, cooperative solutions. As they do so, their primary task will be to identify and tackle the problems affecting European security in their wider context.

This applies particularly to the relationship between the nuclear and conventional dimensions of the European security complex. In Europe the Warsaw Treaty and NATO confront each other with enormous military potentials. The States of the Warsaw Treaty possess a superior conventional potential, which the West perceives as a threat. If all war, be it nuclear or conventional, is to be prevented—and that is our supreme goal—the Western alliance must maintain for the foreseeable future the ability to deter potential aggressors by means of nuclear as well as conventional systems. This deterrence is the main reason why hostilities have not broken out between the Warsaw Treaty and NATO over a period of some 40 years. A comparison with the devastating wars that have been waged outside Europe during the same period speaks for itself. However, the conventional superiority of the Warsaw Treaty should not be used as

---

*Ludger Buerstedde is Chief of the Division for Security, Disarmament, and Arms Control in Europe in the Ministry of Foreign Affairs of the Federal Republic of Germany.

an argument against a balanced and drastic reduction in nuclear arsenals, but rather as an argument for increased efforts to establish stability in the conventional sphere. As an integral element of security policy, arms control must play a major role in achieving conventional stability.

This strong interest in the establishment of a stable and secure balance of conventional forces is in line with the commitment that the Federal Republic of Germany has shown for many years in the conventional field, e.g., at the Vienna Talks on Mutual Reduction of Forces and Armaments and Associated Measures in Central Europe (MBFR) and the Stockholm Conference on Confidence- and Security-building Measures and Disarmament in Europe (CDE). The divide between the alliances passes through the heart of Germany. If a conventional conflict ever broke out in Europe, the Germans in East and West would be the first to suffer. In view of the destructive power of modern conventional weapons, the devastation caused by a conventional war in Central Europe would be inconceivably greater than all the havoc of World War II. Our top priority is therefore the prevention of any war in Europe, nuclear or conventional. This is the goal of our defense efforts as well as of our arms control policy. At the same time, in the conventional field, too, the maxim applies that autonomous defense efforts are not enough to strengthen security; they must be supplemented by cooperative endeavors and, above all, by arms control negotiations.

Important developments are taking place in the field of conventional arms control. For the first time, there are prospects that we shall be able to negotiate about conventional stability in the whole of Europe, from the Atlantic to the Urals. On 17 February, on the initiative of the West, East-West talks began in Vienna with the aim of drawing up a mandate for such negotiations. This development was sparked by the foreign ministers of the North Atlantic Council at their Halifax meeting in May 1986, where, in response to a Franco-German proposal, they committed themselves to new steps toward conventional arms control in the whole of Europe.

The Objective

"Our objective," to quote the Halifax Statement, "is the strengthening of stability and security in the whole of Europe, through increased openness and the establishment of a verifiable, comprehensive and stable balance of conventional forces at lower levels." The ministers then agreed at their autumn meeting in Brussels on a catalogue of principles and criteria for negotiations on the establishment of conventional stability in Europe. The central message of their Brussels Declaration was that "military forces should exist to prevent war and to ensure self-defense, not for the purpose of initiating aggression and not for purposes of political or military intimidation." It follows from this that a long-term goal of the negotiations will be the establishment of conditions in which the security efforts of both sides, in the conventional as well as the nuclear sphere, are directed toward defensive requirements and in which neither side may maintain or lay claim to an offensive capability.

The Present Situation

The situation from which this long-term task is to be approached must, of course, be realistically assessed. The Brussels Declaration says: "Statements by Eastern spokesmen sometimes imply that the present military situation in Europe is stable and balanced. It is not. On the contrary, it is marked by asymmetries and disparities which vary from region to region but which are detrimental to Western security and which are a source of potential instability."

The conventional situation in Europe is effectively characterized by the capability—I do not talk about intentions—of the Warsaw Treaty, with the Soviet Army at its core, to conduct with prospects of success a strategic attack aimed at the occupation of Western Europe. This capability derives from a combination of factors and of advantages enjoyed by the Warsaw Treaty over the NATO in Europe. Together with its allies, the Soviet Union possesses considerable superiority over NATO in Europe in terms of combat-essential heavy weaponry. This superiority prevails both in individual regions of Europe and on the continent as a whole. It is particularly marked in the sphere of major equipment, which, with its high fire-power and mobility, is a fundamental element of offensive capability. This weaponry and its deployment, geared as they are to offensive operability, are the outward manifestations of the Warsaw Treaty's military doctrine, which is based on surprise and attack (i.e., on forcing a decision within the opponent's territory). The Warsaw Treaty's statement of 29 May 1987 regarding the defensive character of its military doctrine is notable. What is vital, however, is that this declared defensiveness be reflected in force sizes and deployment.

In addition, there are the geographical advantages enjoyed by the

Warsaw Treaty. There is little depth between the intra-German boundary and the English Channel or the Atlantic. Western Europe is divided from its main ally, the United States, by the Atlantic, whereas the parties to the Warsaw Treaty are connected with the Soviet Union in one unbroken landmass extending into Soviet Asia. This all means that the Warsaw Treaty has the advantages of greater depth and of direct and secure lines of communication and supply, whereas the territory of NATO is scattered over a long, thin strip from the North Cape to the Aegean Sea.

Finally, the Eastern predilection for excessive secrecy has resulted in a militarily significant lack of transparency. The Stockholm Conference did succeed in adopting a package of measures to improve this situation, which is a good start but insufficient in itself. An increase in information and further measures aimed at creating greater predictability and calculability of military activities are needed.

Ways Toward Stabilization

This analysis shows that the establishment of conventional stability is an immense task. It can be approached only through a step-by-step process of negotiation in which the undiminished security of all concerned is guaranteed at every stage. The States of the Warsaw Treaty and of NATO are agreed on this point. What is essential is that they should agree on the goal of establishing a stable and secure level of forces in conjunction with the elimination of imbalances.

Equal ceilings are a very important and, indeed, essential factor in the establishment of stability, but they are not in themselves sufficient. Consideration must also be given to other relevant factors, such as the deployment, mobility, and operational readiness of military forces, the availability of information about them, and the geostrategic asymmetries outlined above. The prime concern is that the ability to conduct surprise attacks and large-scale offensives should be eliminated. NATO does not possess this invasion capacity.

Unilateral threat options must be removed. Neither side should have reason to fear the other side's ability to conduct an attack, particularly a surprise attack.

Measured against these objectives and criteria, equal linear reductions, as proposed by the Warsaw Treaty in June 1986, are inadequate. They would tend to magnify the existing imbalances instead of reducing them.

Reductions and other measures should be so structured as to reduce offensive capability. To this end, they must lead primarily to a gradual elimination of disparities in the heavy weaponry, which is the basis of offensive capability. A very significant step would be the establishment of equal ceilings at lower levels for combat-essential major equipment such as main battle tanks.

The reduction of imbalances should be accompanied by supplementary measures serving to offset geostrategic asymmetries and to improve transparency, thereby establishing stability. Consideration could be given in this context to deployment constraints and other measures aimed at impeding the conduct of offensive operations and at avoiding circumvention.

The new negotiations on conventional stability are to cover the conventional potentials of the members of both alliances in the whole of Europe. That does not, however, mean that reductions, limitations, or additional constraining measures have to affect all weapons systems and military forces throughout the entire European area of application from the outset. It would make sense to count the forces that actually confront each other. The forces deployed in and designated for specific areas should be compared in accordance with their operational functions. The potentials confronting each other in Central Europe should be dealt with at an early stage of the process. The Soviet forces in forward deployment far beyond the western boundary of the Soviet Union are of particular importance in this respect.

Negotiating Prospects

In their Brussels Declaration of 11 December 1986, the foreign ministers of the North Atlantic Council proposed two distinct sets of negotiations:

First, negotiations among all 35 States participating in the Conference on Security and Co-operation in Europe (CSCE) process to build upon and extend the results of the Stockholm Conference.

Second, negotiations between the 16 members of NATO and the 7 members of the Warsaw Treaty Organization with a view to eliminating existing imbalances in the area between the Atlantic and the Urals and to establishing a conventional balance at lower levels.

The purpose of the East-West talks in Vienna, which were launched on 17 February 1987 as a result of a Western initiative, is to define jointly, in the form of a mandate, the objectives, subject matter, methods, and scope of negotiations on conventional stability in the whole of Europe. In a parallel move, the CSCE follow-up meeting in Vienna should decide in favor of continuing the CDE, so that a further set of confidence- and security-building measures can be negotiated. The two sets of negotiations are interconnected. Further confidence-building measures and the gradual establishment of conventional stability in the whole of Europe are necessary and mutually complementary means of improving the security of all European States. The initiation of such a process of conventional stabilization could become part of the concluding document of the CSCE follow-up meeting in Vienna.

What are the chances of new negotiations on conventional stability in the whole of Europe? Experience of the MBFR negotiations between NATO and the Warsaw Treaty, which have been going on in Vienna since 1973, makes one cautious, particularly in view of the fact that a new approach proposed by the West on 5 December 1985 still awaits a specific response. The prospects will depend upon whether both sides, in particular the Soviet Union, reassess their interests with regard to the balance of conventional forces in Europe, bearing in mind the change of emphasis in foreign, internal, and above all economic policy. No threat of aggression comes from the democracies of NATO; they are interested in the steady development of their economies, and the essential defensive measures to which they limit themselves are taken only because they feel threatened. Is it then worthwhile for the Warsaw Treaty to invest further billions in the maintenance and development of its conventional preponderance, thereby arousing distrust and fear in Western Europe and complicating the search for a basis of peaceful cooperation? Is it not time to channel the available resources into economic development and the promotion of human welfare? Is not such an adjustment the logical consequence of the "new thinking"?

The Warsaw Treaty's statements of 29 May 1987 speak of imbalances and asymmetries on both sides in Europe, arising from historical, geographical, and other factors. They express readiness to eliminate disparities that have developed in some areas; this would be achieved by means of appropriate reductions by the advantaged party. This readiness is significant and should come to fruition in the negotiations on conventional stability, the mandate for which is currently under negotiation by the two sides in Vienna. After all, whoever has more arms must do more disarming.

The negotiations on intermediate-range nuclear forces show that it should be possible to achieve considerably asymmetrical reductions to equal ceilings.

Conventional forces are particularly expensive and a burden on all of us. Their reduction toward a secure and stable balance at the lowest possible levels would release substantial resources for the common good; at the same time, elimination of threatening options and reduction of tensions would permit wide-ranging cooperation between West and East, for which the CSCE process offers an irreplaceable framework. Such cooperation in Europe would also have the necessary beneficial impact beyond the continent on the entire family of nations. We should not wait for the 1990s. The first step along this arduous but promising road should be taken now.

DISARMAMENT IN THE SPHERE OF CONVENTIONAL WEAPONS

*Stefan Murin**

When speaking about the new situation after the Soviet-United States summit meeting in Reykjavik, we have in mind the irreversible impact it has had on the way in which we judge disarmament. We consider the present to be the decisive time for defining the forms and content of negotiations on those new developments not only for the immediate future, but also in the long-term perspective, for the 1990s.

The problem of conventional weapons and conventional disarmament acquires qualitatively new dimensions, especially with respect to the relationship between those weapons and modern means of mass destruction, primarily the nuclear ones, and the role of those two categories of weapons in military doctrines concerning security.

What are the driving forces of conventional armament? If we look at the historical background, we find that after World War II, which brought about the most extensive use of conventional weapons in human history, conventional armaments assumed different positions in different countries.

After nuclear weapons came into being in the United States and, subsequently, a nuclear club was formed, the military-strategic thinking began to focus predominantly on nuclear categories, with conventional armaments and armed forces relegated to a sort of supplementary function. In the West, thinking along those lines made itself felt in the most distinct manner, first, in the concept of massive retaliation based essentially on a crushing nuclear strike. Later on, as new types and systems of nuclear weapons were developed, this doctrine was transformed into the concept of flexible response, envisaging a gradual escalation of nuclear exchange through the use of different kinds of nuclear forces at different stages of a presumed conflict. The common denominator of these two alternatives lies in the concept of nuclear "deterrence," i.e., the claim that it is possible to prevent a war by demonstrating firm determination to use nuclear

---

*Stefan Murin, Vice Minister of Foreign Affairs of Czechoslovakia, was unable to attend the meeting; his paper was presented by Frantisek Penazka, Head of the Department of International Organizations in the Ministry of Foreign Affairs.

weapons. Lately, in referring to an alleged threat of conventional attack by Warsaw Treaty member States, the West has mentioned nuclear deterrence with increasing frequency.

Moreover, it is paradoxical that whereas, on the global scale, conventional armament holds in military-strategic doctrines a supplementary position in relation to nuclear weapons, it nevertheless consumes about 80 percent of the world's military spending and constitutes the main source of the constant increase in military budgets. According to the most modest estimates, the world's arsenal of conventional weapons includes over 140,000 main battle tanks, more than 35,000 combat airplanes, 21,000 helicopters, 1,100 large surface warships, and 700 attack submarines. A considerable part of these arms expenditures is devoted to maintaining the world's armed forces, which, according to some estimates, number about 25 million men. It becomes obvious that in Western economies, conventional armament remains—even under the changed historical conditions—the mainstay of the military-industrial complex and its most lucrative component, producing four-fifths of the total profit.

Conventional weapons occupy a dominant position in the security-related considerations of those States that do not possess nuclear weapons, especially of those that are not tied to nuclear powers by politico-military agreements. The Third World countries, confronted with the remnants and consequences of colonial conflicts and exploitation, are compelled, for both objective and subjective reasons, to strive to obtain the most sophisticated conventional weapons available, while facing the gravest danger of their use.

During the past 42 years, over 20 million people have perished in more than 150 local armed conflicts. This number exceeds the number of soldiers killed in World War II. The conflicts have taken place on the territories of more than 70 States, primarily developing ones, and over one-half of all United Nations Member States have been involved in them. As a proportion of national income, the expenditures of developing countries on conventional armaments and armed forces are substantially—in some cases several times—higher than those in advanced countries. (Altogether, the military spending of developing countries constitutes almost one-fifth of total military expenditures.) This alone further aggravates their economic underdevelopment and exacerbates the crisis in the world economy and the instability resulting therefrom.

Producers and Consumers

It thus appears that the role of conventional weapons varies among countries, which may be producers or consumers. The consumers include, naturally, both those who buy weapons on the world market, i.e., primarily developing countries, and the armed forces of the producer States. The producers, whose political, economic, and strategic position depends upon the state of the development of conventional weapons, often view Third World countries as convenient test sites for their weapons.

This process, which has been going on, practically undisturbed, for more than 40 years, has inherent, conflicting tendencies that were almost indiscernible in its initial stages, but that are now growing in importance and are changing its quality.

The establishment of a military-strategic balance, the consequent impossibility of waging a victorious nuclear war, and the application of scientific and technological advances in the development of conventional weapons have resulted in a great lessening of the difference between conventional armaments and weapons of mass destruction and may lead to their total elimination. Development is proceeding with a view to producing entirely new generations of high-precision types of homing missiles built on the basis of new physical principles (radio waves, laser, or infrasound) and of genetic and biophysical principles. Armies are being equipped with weapons based on highly sophisticated technologies, such as FAE (fuel air explosive) munition, electromagnetic guns with high rates of fire, laser weapons for tactical use, guided missiles, highly sophisticated tactical aircraft, and remotely piloted vehicles with reconnaissance and attack capabilities.

In the context of the present and, even more, of the future, this situation leads us inevitably to two fundamental and interrelated conclusions:

First, it becomes difficult to distinguish between an armed conflict involving the use of conventional weapons and the beginning of a nuclear war; the probability of the escalation of any conflict into a global catastrophe and the risk of conflict in general are growing rapidly.

Second, if that is the case, then the justification of the concept of nuclear deterrence—that it prevents one horrible occurrence (war) by posing a threat of an even greater horror (nuclear apocalypse)—ceases to be valid.

In this respect, too, it is correct to conclude that the issue of war and peace has now acquired an entirely new meaning and that it requires a new way of thinking about achieving jointly guaranteed security by non-military, i.e., political, means. It is also evident that the problem of conventional disarmament, just as that of disarmament in the nuclear field, requires a global approach to all its aspects. Naturally, it has to be understood that what is needed above all is a reduction of armed forces and conventional armaments in Europe, where there is the highest concentration of those weapons. In this respect, one can learn a lesson from the evolution of approaches to nuclear disarmament.

The use of nuclear weapons toward the end of World War II, which resulted in the tragedies of Hiroshima and Nagasaki, marked the beginning of four decades of an increasingly intensive nuclear arms buildup, which has produced a destructive and hardly controllable force capable of destroying human civilization several times over. In my opinion, the danger of nuclear destruction was highlighted in particularly strong terms by the Chernobyl accident, an event that could not fail to affect Europeans' views of the possible use of nuclear weapons and that is evidence of the fact that even the most sophisticated technology is not entirely safe from the risk of breakdown or human error.

At the same time, numerous responsible officials have begun to realize, to an ever greater extent, what the consequences would be if conventional weapons alone were used in the densely populated areas of Europe against chemical plants or nuclear power stations. The result of an attack on such facilities, whether accidental or intentional, would be practically equal to the effect of the use of nuclear weapons. Conventional weapons systems are not subject to any limitations like those that are applied, to a certain extent, to nuclear weapons; therefore, they constitute a potentially highly destabilizing factor.

We thus face the need to make a momentous political decision: whether to prevent, through a new, global approach and effective regional measures, a qualitatively new stage of conventional armament (new in content and scope and in respect of the conditions under which it would take place) or to open the door wide to overall military-strategic destabilization. The latter would naturally entail paying the grave political, economic, and social price of a new conventional arms buildup. An awareness of that consequence may have recently aroused worries in some Western European governments about giving up the relatively less expensive nuclear weapons on their territories and replacing them with intensified conventional armament, as was unambiguously demanded of them from overseas.

At present, there thus are two different approaches to issues of peace and security and to the overall problem of disarmament. The first includes the so-called Strategic Defense Initiative (SDI), which is not a means of doing away with nuclear weapons, but a nuclear system of the fourth generation, which will surpass all the systems that have existed until now (atomic, hydrogen, and neutron) by moving atomic radiation to outer space and directing its destructive power to targets on Earth.

In the sphere of conventional weapons, the strategic concept of "follow-on forces attack" (FOFA), known as the Rogers doctrine, was approved by NATO toward the end of 1984 and offensive arms for its implementation have been developed. This doctrine envisages rearming NATO forces by supplying them with new conventional weapons and systems comparable in some respects to weapons of mass destruction. Those armaments—bombers, missiles, devices for detection of and guidance toward targets—are destined for operations to be carried out as far as 500 kilometers deep into the territory of the Socialist states. The concept supposes that NATO armed forces would be grouped in a way that would enable them to launch a conventional war involving, from the very beginning, large-scale offensive operations that would take place on the territory of Socialist countries.

Grave concerns have also been aroused by NATO's decisions and plans adopted at its session of ministers of defense in May 1986. Those plans, which aim to obtain the capability of a first strike, envisage enhancement of conventional armament and extensive modernization of the equipment of armies.

The second approach to issues of peace and security is evident in the attitude of the Socialist countries. Their military doctrine is based on different considerations, primarily on the premise that in the present circumstances it is inadmissible to settle any question by military means. Their guiding principle is that genuine security can be provided for in all spheres of international relations only by political means, on the basis of equality for all. This is the objective underlying their proposal for establishing a comprehensive system of international peace and security, which they put forward in the United Nations in 1986 and which has been receiving great attention worldwide.

At the recently concluded session of the Political Consultative Committee of the Warsaw Treaty member States in Berlin, the participating countries reaffirmed that their alliance was of a peaceful nature and that their military doctrine pursued solely defensive purposes. They proposed that the two alliances hold consultations as soon as possible to compare their military doctrines, to analyze the character of those doctrines, and to consider jointly their future direction with a view to doing away with mutual suspicion and mistrust, increasing mutual understanding, and ensuring that they would be based on defensive principles.

In proposing talks on those issues, the member States of the Warsaw Treaty were responding directly to those Western European politicians who have displayed strong concerns about claims that considerable conventional instability would result if nuclear weapons were eliminated.

It should be emphasized that the member States of the Warsaw Treaty, desirous of creating the best possible conditions for future negotiations, have declared their readiness to exercise, on the basis of reciprocity, the utmost restraint in the development of their military potentials. This would include the nonincrease of armed forces and conventional armaments and also the adoption for one to two years of a moratorium on increases in military expenditures.

As far as verification is concerned, we have proposed, in addition to strict and comprehensive verification measures relating to the process of reductions in conventional armaments and armed forces, to introduce observation of the activities of the troops that would remain in place after the reductions. These measures, together with the exchange of data on armed forces and armaments of all participating States and other international procedures, including on-site inspections, would ensure reliable and effective compliance with the adopted obligations.

A significant step would be taken by implementing the Budapest program of the Warsaw Treaty countries, issued in June 1986. That program envisages the elimination of Warsaw Treaty and NATO military bases in the territories of other countries and the reciprocal withdrawals of troops to their respective national territories. It also calls for immediate reductions in armed forces and conventional armaments in the whole of Europe—from the Atlantic to the Urals—to be made in stages until a level of reasonable adequacy, i.e., the level needed for the fulfilment of tasks of defense, is reached. Imbalances and asymmetries in individual kinds of weapons, determined by historical and geopolitical factors, should be eliminated through reductions on the side that has an advantage. The Socialist States act on the basis of the fact that there is an overall balance in the Warsaw Treaty and NATO forces in Europe, with 3 million men on each side.

The States parties to the Warsaw Treaty propose that in the first stage (one to two years), the troops on each side be reduced by 100,000 to 150,000 men. In the next stage, in the early 1990s, the ground forces and tactical air forces in all of Europe would be reduced by 25 percent, compared to their present level. The number of troops of the two sides facing each other in Europe would thus be decreased by more than a million men, with the greatest reductions being made in the concentration of troops and armaments in the zone of direct contact between the Warsaw Treaty and NATO. Both sides would also withdraw the most dangerous and offensive kinds of weapons from this zone. The process of reductions would then continue, with the participation of the other European States as well.

The proposal envisages the process of reductions on the basis of reciprocity, with the balance of power being maintained. This would be conducive to strengthening military-strategic stability. Reductions would be made in all components of ground forces and attack air forces, all armaments and technical combat equipment organically belonging to the respective units, including tactical nuclear weapons. Thus the negotiations would also cover the so-called short-range nuclear forces, which are mostly dual-capable weapons (able to carry both conventional and nuclear warheads) and which have not been the subject of any negotiations thus far. The contractual obligations of the parties would include, as an integral part, the exchange of information on exercises and movements of troops and a comprehensive system of both national and international verification, including on-site inspections.

In the Budapest Appeal, the Socialist States adopted a highly flexible attitude concerning the question of where and how to resolve the problem of the reduction of armed forces and conventional armaments on our continent. The Political Consultative Committee's session in Berlin reaffirmed that the best forum for talks on those issues would be the second stage of the Conference on Confidence- and Security-building Measures and Disarmament in Europe. They also expressed readiness to consider other alternatives within the framework of the all-European process, including the convening of a special forum. The Socialist States have proposed convening a meeting of the ministers of foreign affairs of all states participating in the Conference on Security and Co-operation in Europe in order to open extensive negotiations on radical reductions in armed forces, conventional armaments, and tactical nuclear weapons in Europe and adequate reductions in military expenditures.

In the Brussels Declaration, the NATO States declared verbally their readiness "to open East-West discussions with a view to the establishment of a new mandate for negotiating on conventional arms control covering the whole of Europe from the Atlantic to the Urals," yet until now they have not confirmed that readiness in practice at the consultations in

Vienna. Because of lack of willingness on their part, it has been impossible to start actual work on the mandate for future negotiations.

As we see the situation, the consultations on conventional disarmament being conducted by 23 European States have mainly revealed that the NATO States are still not willing to negotiate on radical reductions in armed forces and armaments. They speak only about safeguarding "conventional stability" and doing away with what they assert to be an imbalance that places the West at a disadvantage in Europe as a whole and also in particular areas.

It should be emphasized that raising the problem of conventional disarmament on an all-European scale does not mean that the Socialist countries are losing interest in progress and tangible results at the Vienna Talks on Mutual Reduction of Forces and Armaments and Associated Measures in Central Europe. We attach great importance to these talks, especially since disarmament measures adopted there would cover the territory of Central Europe, which, though limited in size, is of extreme significance. They would help to thin out forces located in the zone of direct contact between the Warsaw Treaty and NATO, i.e., the area with the greatest concentration of manpower and the most sophisticated combat equipment.

Since the beginning of those talks in October 1973, the Socialist States have put forward 28 compromise proposals of either a global or partial nature. Two proposals are on the negotiating table at present: the position of the NATO States of 5 December 1985 and the draft "Agreement on an initial cutback by the Soviet Union and the United States in land forces and armaments with a subsequent non-increase in the levels of the armed forces and armaments of the sides and related measures in Central Europe," put forward by the States members of the Warsaw Treaty on 20 February 1986 and further elaborated by them in the course of the talks held pursuant to the Final Document of the Stockholm Conference.

Although the positions of the two sides have since become very close or even identical on many points, the Western participants do not appear willing to seek compromise solutions to the outstanding issues. They persist in refusing to negotiate on reductions and limitations of armaments. They are not willing to finalize the scope and form of the initial reduction of Soviet and United States ground forces, and, most importantly, they strive for adoption of inappropriate associated and verification measures that would not correspond, either in scope or in content, to the disarmament measures to be adopted.

Even in this complicated situation, we are ready to continue to work for progress at those talks and to seek a way out that would create favorable conditions for transition to talks on reducing armed forces and conventional armaments on an all-European scale.

Stability in Europe might also be significantly enhanced through the implementation of Poland's plan, submitted on 8 May 1987, for limiting armaments and building confidence in Central Europe. This plan offers Central Europe a clear prospect: the elimination of nuclear weapons accompanied by removal of the most dangerous and most offensive types of conventional weapons from the region, the simultaneous expansion of confidence- and security-building measures and strict verification, and mutual recognition of the purely defensive nature of both alliances' military doctrines. The proposals for establishing nuclear and chemical weapons-free zones in Central Europe, the Balkans, and Northern Europe would also be conducive to reducing military confrontation and strengthening security in parts of Europe.

The governments of Czechoslovakia and the German Democratic Republic have also proposed establishing a nuclear weapon-free corridor in Central Europe that would extend 150 kilometers on each side of the border between Czechoslovakia and the Federal Republic of Germany and between the German Democratic Republic and the Federal Republic of Germany. The proposal envisages reciprocal withdrawal from the corridor of all nuclear weapons: nuclear munitions, including nuclear mines, tactical missiles, nuclear artillery, and nuclear-capable ground attack aircraft, and also antiaircraft and antimissile defense complexes that might carry nuclear weapons. A considerable part of those weapons consists in dual-capable arms. It is our opinion that establishment of the proposed corridor might also accelerate the solution of the question of reducing armed forces and conventional armaments in Europe.

The Socialist countries adhere to the basic principle that disarmament in the sphere of conventional weapons has to be carried out together with nuclear disarmament and the elimination of all other kinds of weapons of mass destruction, primarily chemical ones. They also consider that States possessing nuclear weapons and other countries with major military potentials, especially members of politico-military groupings, have a special responsibility in this regard. However, in reality, the reduction of armed forces and conventional armaments to a level that would be reasonably adequate for defense and safeguarding every State's right to security is a matter of global impact, affecting all regions.

To formulate a global approach to the questions of conventional disarmament and to activate the United Nations for that purpose is thus truly topical. This was the premise of the Socialist proposal recently submitted to the United Nations Disarmament Commission. It called on all member States to work by all means available for success in negotiations on conventional weapons in accordance with agreed principles and to refrain from steps that would impede progress in that direction.

In conclusion, I should like to stress that there is a real prospect for progress, made possible primarily by the flexible approach of the Socialist countries to the problem of conventional forces and armaments. What is needed here, just as in the nuclear field, is the capacity to abandon obsolete stereotyped patterns of thought based on the pursuit of individual or group interests through military strength. Also needed is a new attitude toward achieving collectively agreed upon priorities in the disarmament field, primarily universal recognition of the fact that the problem of conventional disarmament, too, is now a global problem of our interrelated and interdependent world. It is obvious that this new way of thinking has been growing in strength; if this trend continues, it will produce results beneficial for all.

DISARMAMENT IN THE FIELD OF CONVENTIONAL WEAPONS AND CONFIDENCE-BUILDING MEASURES

*Sigrid Pöllinger**

When you conferred on me the honor of addressing this important international forum on disarmament, I did not realize how difficult the task would be. I had expected to analyze the Vienna Talks on Mutual Reduction of Forces and Armaments and Associated Measures in Central Europe (M(B)FR), their achievements and failures, and the efforts being undertaken at present in Vienna to create a new forum for conventional disarmament talks covering the whole continent of Europe.

However, in the meantime the rather static scene has come into motion, so it will be difficult to pass any definitive judgment. For that, you would have to be a prophet, and I certainly do not claim to possess such powers. Nevertheless, I will try to live up to the challenge to the best of my ability. I take this liberty for three reasons: first, as an Austrian; second, as a representative of a peace research institution; and third, as a woman.

Since Austria is a neutral country in the heart of Europe, it has a particular interest in the safeguarding of peace and its corollary, disarmament. Austria is not a military superpower, and in any major military confrontation could not escape untouched by virtue of neutrality alone, although it is certainly significant that Vienna, my home town, is not only the third United Nations city, but also one of the major venues of disarmament talks. In the case of conventional weapons, of which I will talk in greater detail later, I don't think I have to elaborate on the significance of peace research institutions and the interest women in general have always had in the maintenance of peace. I have a famous compatriot, Bertha von Suttner, who was awarded the Nobel Peace Prize for organizing effective disarmament campaigns already at the turn of the century. The title of her book *Put Down Your Arms* is as potent today as it was then.

I think we cannot plan for the future if we do not first look back into the past, even if this presents a depressing picture. After all, disarmament

---

*Sigrid Pöllinger is professor at the University Centre for Peace Research in Vienna, Austria.

talks are not a postwar phenomenon. They started at the beginning of the century, but were not able to prevent the two world wars. Ever since the end of World War II, disarmament negotiations have been going on—mainly in two cities of neutral European countries, Geneva and Vienna—not with overwhelming success. In Geneva on 2 June, the United States and the USSR agreed in principle on a common draft to eliminate medium-range missiles in Europe. This is a hopeful development, which may lead to a breakthrough. In this connection, I want to stress the importance of the potential influence of public opinion—including that of disarmament campaigns—in shaping disarmament policies. In Vienna we are now at a crossroads with respect to conventional disarmament.

I personally consider the negotiations covering conventional weapons particularly significant. After all, more than 40 years after the end of hostilities in Europe, we are still faced with the biggest concentration of troops and armaments that has ever existed in peace time in a relatively small geographic area. Furthermore, even if the two superpowers have become pivots of world politics, Europe has remained the strategic center of East-West confrontation. Of the approximately $800 billion spent worldwide on armaments, about 70 percent is used for the NATO and Warsaw Treaty forces. Furthermore, the costs of the conventional arms race are proportionally far higher than those of the nuclear arms race.

In the early 1970s, the capacity for overkill led to the realization that a potential conflict could no longer be solved by military means. The necessity of coming to an understanding produced a series of conferences, of which I consider the most important to be the so-called Helsinki process. It started in the Finnish capital in 1973 and led to the signing of the Final Act two years later. Directly linked politically to that conference and concurrent with it were the Vienna Talks, which opened, on 30 October 1973 to be exact, with associated measures as an integral part of their mandate. Those talks are still in progress. Thus a process was set in motion that knows no precedent in history. Never before had representatives of two opposing military alliances agreed to sit down in peace time with the aim of reaching an understanding on reducing their armed forces. Even then nobody expected a quick breakthrough, but it was generally thought that the success or failure of the endeavor would become visible in the foreseeable future. Instead, we are now faced with the 42nd round and the 450th plenary session. For 10 years the two sides were deadlocked on two major issues: the data question and the problem of verification. As for the data question, the East insisted that a balance of forces already existed, whereas the West maintained that the Warsaw Treaty forces were in fact larger. As for verification, the controversy centered on the question of where and how verification should take place.

It was only in the tenth year of the negotiations that things began to move. On 18 February 1982, the East for the first time presented the draft of a complete agreement, to which the West replied with its own concept on 25 November. Although the two sides were still wide apart, the mere fact that draft agreements had been submitted was regarded as a sign of a positive development. The task became to unite the two drafts into a common accord. Unfortunately, it turned out that the two sides would not move from their positions and thus no compromise seemed possible for the time being.

This deadlock persisted until 5 December 1985, when the NATO countries dropped their insistence that the sides come to a common understanding on force levels before they agreed to initial reductions of forces and the no-increase commitment, thus removing the so-called data barrier to any progress. At the same time, the West stressed the importance of verification, which, it maintained, was vital to any agreement. First, it held that verification should consist of permanently manned sites through which all forces of the participating countries entering or leaving Central Europe must pass. Second, the West insisted on a detailed exchange of information on forces, down to battalion level, thus establishing a basis for verifying the no-increase commitment. Finally, the NATO countries suggested that each side should have the right to conduct 30 inspections per year during each of the three years of reductions. On 20 February 1986, the Warsaw Treaty countries submitted their reply in the form of a draft agreement, which, although accepting the common ground, departed from the Western view as far as verification was concerned. With regard to on-site inspection, the Warsaw Treaty countries maintained that in every case justification must first be given to the country to be inspected. There the matter rests at present.

The Helsinki meeting—as you all know—had two follow-up meetings. The first was held in Belgrade from 1977 to 1978, and the second in Madrid from 1980 to 1983. It was in Madrid that for the first time within this framework steps were taken that had a direct bearing on the question of disarmament. I am referring to the Stockholm Conference on Confidence- and Security-building Measures and Disarmament in Europe, which received its mandate from the Madrid meeting and which concluded on 19 September 1986 with the adoption of a document, the first to be agreed upon since the Helsinki Final Act. The Stockholm Document referred to several measures designed to reduce tension in Europe. First, with regard to the threat or use of force, the participating States reaffirm their commitment to refrain from the threat or use of force in their relations with any State, regardless of that State's political, social, economic, or cultural system and irrespective of whether or not they maintain with the State relations of alliance. Second, with regard to the notification of military maneuvers, such activities involving between 13,000 and 40,000 men have to be notified one year in advance and those with over 40,000, two years in advance. Maneuvers involving more than 75,000 men must not take place, unless announced two years previously. Third, with regard to observation, two observers have to be invited for all exercises involving more than 17,000 men. Fourth, with regard to verification, any country that doubts the observance of the agreement by another State has the right to demand an on-site inspection, which must not be refused.

The Stockholm accord was the rare instance of a document that was welcomed by all sides. According to most observers, the document surpassed the expectations of even fervent optimists, not so much for its content as for the confidence it was designed to create.

In the meantime, another round of consultations has developed in Vienna, this time on an informal basis. The participants are the 23 members of the two military alliances, who have been meeting alternately at an Eastern or Western embassy in Vienna. The difference between these consultations and the M(B)FR framework is that (1) France, not represented at M(B)FR, is participating in the talks, and (2) the area of force reductions would not cover Central Europe alone, but the entire continent from the Atlantic to the Urals, including the Mediterranean area. The participants in the "Talks of the 23" are at the same time the representatives of their countries to the current follow-up meeting in Vienna of the Conference on Security and Co-operation in Europe (CSCE). The main question now is whether conventional disarmament should stay out of the CSCE or be linked more closely with the Helsinki process.

And this brings me to the point that, I freely admit, is closest to my heart and that has for a long time been a special field in my research work—the question of confidence and confidence-building measures.

In considering the failure of disarmament negotiations, we have to ask the question: Could it be that the whole mode of negotiating has been wrong? Efforts for peace and disarmament have concentrated so far on reaching treaties in order to reduce the level of troops and armaments. The results have been meager. What has happened appears to me like an attempt to do away with the symptoms of the arms race without looking at the underlying causes, which are fear and mistrust. Without a study of these causes, disarmament efforts are liable to lead nowhere and end in failure. This seems to me like an attempt to put the cart before the horse or to fight against the fever and not the illness. The only way out of this dilemma is to create an atmosphere of confidence on different levels. Confidence may not be everything, but without mutual confidence there can be no progress. The historical record confirms my contention.

What kind of confidence-building measures are essential? We should distinguish between two types: first, political and psychological measures and, second, practical or contractually agreed upon measures.

With regard to political and psychological measures, we are faced with the necessity of undertaking what one could describe as "disarmament of words." At present, words that are hostile to the purpose of peace and disarmament are used in the peace dialogue and conferences. Speeches by representatives—not only those of the two superpowers, but also of other nations—are deliberately directed at the faults and weaknesses of the other party. There must be more voluntary restraint. Nations should try to talk to each other and not against each other. This means that the other party's point of view should never be rejected out of hand. One should always try to understand the other party's case or there can be no progress. Where should the "disarmament of words" begin? I suggest it should start in all international forums, above all in those of the United Nations, because there is no better place for building confidence among nations than the United Nations, and particularly its disarmament conferences. We cannot have confidence in someone whom we do not know. We have to come to know each other. Confidence-building is absolutely essential if we are aiming at disarmament and a life of peace and security.

Another possible way of building confidence would be to encourage the extension of peace research in East and West. I would suggest, as a concrete step for a confidence-building measure, that one-tenth of 1 percent of the money spent on the arms race be diverted to peace research. Unfortunately, there is little confidence between nations. From personal experience I can say that peace researchers in East and West do have considerable trust in and mutual respect for each other when dealing with concrete problems such as disarmament. Universities worldwide should put more emphasis on peace education. Classes on peace and disarmament should be introduced in East and West. The exchange of students, assistants, and professors should be encouraged.

As for the practical confidence-building measures, their importance was stressed in the Final Document of the first special session on disarmament. Thus the United Nations followed the example adopted by the Final Act of the CSCE in Helsinki, which approved a whole series of confidence-building measures of the so-called first generation. These measures dealt mainly with military topics. Generally speaking, they have been implemented by both sides and have thus contributed to the building of a minimum of confidence, which would serve as a basis for further steps.

I have now reached what I think is the logical conclusion, the crux of the matter: disarmament alone, however much we all may wish for it, will not lead to confidence among nations. Rather, it is confidence-building measures that will pave the road to disarmament, and this road is the surest road to security and peace.

REYKJAVIK AND MILITARY ASPECTS OF EUROPEAN SECURITY

*Wojciech Multan**

At no other Soviet-American summit meeting has so much attention been devoted to European questions as at the Gorbachev-Reagan working meeting in the capital of Iceland. Also, at none of them have such important understandings been reached, which directly concern the most vital security interests of European nations. For these reasons, it seems worthwhile to have a look at the meeting of the Soviet and United States leaders in Reykjavik and ask the question: What has it meant for Europe?

The Reykjavik meeting took place several months after the USSR had presented a three-stage program for eliminating weapons of mass destruction by the year 2000 and after a wide-ranging discussion of the idea of common security in the course of preparations for and during the debates of the Twenty-seventh Congress of the Communist Party of the Soviet Union (CPSU). The Soviet leader proposed the summit meeting because he wished to express the USSR's concern about the continuing arms race, on the one hand, and lack of progress in disarmament dialogue, on the other, and to give a strong impulse to Soviet-American negotiations on the most important aspects of the present arms race. Moreover, on the initiative of the American side, the participants in that meeting discussed questions of human rights in international relations, regional conflicts, and Soviet-American bilateral issues. According to the accounts of both sides, however, disarmament problems occupied the central place.[1]

We are interested here only in the suggestions put forward concerning the European continent. Very briefly speaking, they envisaged the adoption by both sides of the following understandings on this subject: In the three-part package of proposals, which provided for a 50 percent reduction in offensive strategic systems and a 10-year prohibition on renouncing the antiballistic missile (ABM) Treaty—including a prohibition on carrying out tests within the SDI program—there was a proposal for

---

*Wojciech Multan is Deputy Director of the Polish Institute for International Affairs in Warsaw.

completely eliminating American and Soviet medium-range nuclear weapons in Europe and for freezing the present number of short-range nuclear weapons. The American side raised no objections to these proposals at the meeting.[2] Besides, the Soviet Union suggested starting negotiations on the complete prohibition of nuclear weapon tests, reinforcing its proposal by further extending its unilateral moratorium.

The formula that the Soviet side presented in Reykjavik and according to which the two global powers were to begin removing their nuclear weapons from the European continent constituted a major concession to the United States; it signified acceptance of the "zero option" presented by Reagan in 1981. The most important element of this concession was that Moscow would exclude the British and French nuclear potentials from the total calculation of East-West nuclear forces in Europe. As you know, those potentials are considerable and will be even greater after the present programs of development have been completed.[3] Moreover, the NATO potential in Europe would include: American F-111 nuclear bombers stationed in the United Kingdom; nearly 300 Pluton, Pershing I, and Lance missiles; and over 3,000 nuclear artillery warheads.[4]

Following the presentation of these general ideas in Reykjavik, the two sides submitted at the Geneva negotiations in March and April 1987 concretely formulated proposals for Soviet-American agreements on eliminating medium-range nuclear weapons from Europe. At this point, divergencies and difficulties appeared. The draft agreement submitted in Geneva by the Soviet delegation provided for also eliminating from Europe tactical-operational weapons with a range of 500–1,000 kilometers. The American side suggested that the USSR freeze weapons of this type at the present level and that the United States expand its potential by modifying the already deployed Pershing II and Tomahawk missiles. The modification would consist in shortening the range of Pershing II missiles and transferring Tomahawk missiles to ships or aircraft. In other words, the USSR would be expected to agree to a very disadvantageous operation, because it is fairly generally accepted that the previous range of these missiles could be relatively easily restored. The argument that the Western side does not command an appropriate category of weapons is not entirely true. I think, however, that with a minimum of goodwill on the part of the West—not only the United States, but also the other members of NATO—it will be possible to find a way out. I believe that prospects for completely eliminating medium-range nuclear weapons from Europe and for at least reducing to a considerable extent the number of weapons with a range of below 1,000 kilometers will grow brighter. This would constitute indisputable proof of the contribution that the Reykjavik meeting has made to European security.

I believe that the meeting of the Soviet and United States leaders in the capital of Iceland should be viewed more broadly. It should be considered in the context of possibilities for other agreements concerning military aspects of European security and for definite proposals submitted in another forum. I refer here in particular to the agreements reached at the Stockholm Conference on Confidence- and Security-building Measures and Disarmament in Europe, which ended on 19 September 1986, and the readiness of the States parties to the Warsaw Treaty to take up negotiations on limiting conventional armed forces and armaments in Europe.[5]

The Stockholm Conference achieved significant progress on the very important question of military confidence-building measures. The Document of the Conference provides for far-reaching steps, of both a substantive and territorial nature, in this field. At the moment, the delegates of 35 States are negotiating in Vienna on a mandate for the second phase of the Conference. There are chances that the mandate will encompass possibilities for negotiating both a third generation of confidence-building measures and concrete steps aimed at limiting armed forces and armaments. The weekly meetings in Vienna of representatives of the 23 States parties to the Warsaw Treaty and NATO should be helpful in working out a realistic program that will meet the expectations of the European public for multilateral negotiations on all aspects of security and cooperation in Europe.

A unique situation is emerging, in which all the military aspects of security in Europe will soon become the subject of negotiations. This development will concern every kind of nuclear weapon, conventional armed forces and armaments, and confidence-building measures. There will be no "gray zone" weapons, i.e., systems not embraced by any negotiations or remaining outside any international agreements. Naturally, taking up negotiations on a definite question does not guarantee reaching an agreement. However, this is the prelude, without which the finale would be impossible.

Thus we can speak of a continuation of Reykjavik with respect to Europe. The implementation of the vision outlined at the Gorbachev-Reagan meeting with respect to Europe should create a favorable basis for harmonizing negotiations on the main questions relative to military aspects of European security.

It is natural to ask at this point: What would be the appropriate forum for negotiations? Matters pertaining directly to the question of eliminating nuclear weapons should remain in the hands of the two superpowers —at least until France and the United Kingdom join in the talks in order to create a global "nuclear order." Of course, this does not preclude the possibility of nonnuclear States taking up the question of setting up a nuclear-free zone in a definite region. Such negotiations would be highly desirable and should there be success in Soviet-American talks on eliminating nuclear weapons from Europe, the chances for their success would significantly increase.

The question of negotiations on limiting conventional armed forces and armaments is somewhat complicated. The experience of the 19 States parties to the Warsaw Treaty and NATO that have been conducting negotiations in Vienna since 1973 has not been very encouraging. For several months now, the delegates of 23 States representing the two military-political groupings have been meeting in the same capital to seek agreement on the subject matter and the forum of negotiations on conventional disarmament for all of Europe. Two opposing views on the forum of negotiations have been expressed. The Socialist countries suggest that the question be examined during the second phase of the Conference of 35 States in Stockholm. The NATO States, however, consider that the problem should be taken up in the forum of 23 States members of the military alliances. I think that a compromise solution is possible, one satisfactory to the three groups of States that determine the political-military climate on our continent.

If a situation develops that is conducive to holding comprehensive negotiations on military aspects of European security, it will be necessary to work out a coherent program embracing all the basic questions relating to the concept and practical content of military détente. In the past, on Finland's initiative, attempts were made to elaborate such a program. Unfortunately, they ended in failure because the overall political atmosphere of East-West relations was unfavorable at that time. If there is a success in the Soviet-American talks in Geneva on medium-range nuclear weapons and if multilateral negotiations on the remaining questions begin, the idea of elaborating such a program should be well received. The program should reflect the idea of the common security of all 35 States participating in the CSCE (Conference on Security and Cooperation in Europe) process. There is no need to prove that the significance of general European solutions in the field of military aspects of security would go far beyond the continent, greatly contributing to the stabilization of international relations on a global scale.

Thus, in my opinion, the reply to the question at the beginning of the paper should be, in brief, that the Soviet-American summit meeting in Reykjavik has contributed toward clarifying standpoints on the fundamental question of the gradual elimination of nuclear weapons from Europe. It has defined the basic formula of a future Soviet-American agreement on the complete elimination of medium-range nuclear weapons (1,000–5,000-kilometer range). It has made it possible to formulate the initial positions of the two sides on the possibility of reaching agreement on short-range nuclear weapons, i.e., tactical operational missiles with a 500–1,000-kilometer range, and to outline the form of negotiations on tactical nuclear systems with a range of less than 500 kilometers. Thus a convenient starting point has been provided for a broader dialogue on reducing conventional forces in Europe. The periodic meetings of representatives of 23 States in Vienna and the discussions in the Vienna 1986 forum between representatives of the 35 States signatories to the CSCE Final Act seem to confirm this presupposition.

Thus Reykjavik has furnished the point of departure for a comprehensive program of activity embracing all the basic military aspects of European security. The political climate created by this summit meeting is also auspicious for submitting and implementing subregional solutions concerning military aspects of security on our continent, including the plan, put forward by Poland on 8 May 1987, for the gradual disengagement and reduction of armaments and for new security- and confidence-building measures in the territories of nine States in Central Europe.

The meeting in Reykjavik also invites a more detailed discussion of the problem of military doctrines and their regional and global aspects. Such discussions should take place among representatives of both political-military blocs. A careful analysis of Warsaw Treaty and NATO operative military doctrines that will allow each side to recognize the other's doctrine as defensive should provide interesting material for studies on future concepts of international security in general. These discussions would enable us to understand better the often repeated thesis that no country—even if it allocates the most extensive resources—is able to guarantee its own security.

Notes

1. The Soviet and American accounts of the meeting in Reykjavik tally on this question. See the following two articles published in *Disarmament*, vol. X, No. 1

(winter 1986/1987): Aleksandr Bessmertnykh, "Window on a nuclear-free world," and Rozanne L. Ridgway, "United States-Soviet relations after Reykjavik."

2. Several days after the meeting, the United States put forward the following postulates with respect to the existing proposals for eliminating medium-range nuclear systems: (*a*) part of the United States medium-range missiles should be left in Europe; (*b*) the United States would retain the right to "additional" armament as regards missiles with a range of 500–1,000 kilometers; (*c*) the United States would deploy 100 nuclear warheads in Alaska.

3. This potential now includes 162 nuclear delivery vehicles with some 400 warheads, and it is planned to increase the number of warheads to 1,200 in the early 1990s. In the case of the United Kingdom, the modernization is to consist of replacing Polaris submarines carrying 16 missile launchers aboard with Trident submarines carrying 24 launchers aboard. In the case of France, the modernization would consist of equipping submarines with M-4 missile launchers. See *The Military Balance: 1986–1987* (London: IISS, 1986), pp. 57–60, 63–67.

4. See *Newsweek*, 27 April 1987.

5. A program for reducing the conventional potentials of NATO and the Warsaw Treaty was presented at the meeting of the Warsaw Treaty's Political Consultative Committee in Budapest in June 1986 (A/41/411-S/18147).

Chapter 2

Nuclear Weapons

TOWARD NUCLEAR ARMS LIMITATION AND GLOBAL DISARMAMENT AFTER REYKJAVIK

*Tunde Adeniran**

The Reykjavik summit between General Secretary Mikhail Gorbachev and President Ronald Reagan in October 1986 has been described as "a planetary watershed."[1] The Hofdi House deliberations could have turned out to be that, but for some post-Reykjavik incidents that call for caution in the assessment of likely future developments. Only a year before Reykjavik, its antecedents and the terse exchanges between the American and Soviet administrations had led one prominent scholar in modern strategy to conclude that "the possibilities of complete nuclear disarmament by negotiation or unilateral actions look immensely remote. For an indefinite period ahead, mankind is condemned to live under the shadow of the nuclear bomb."[2] But Reykjavik raised hopes for the prevention of nuclear war, the cessation of nuclear weapon tests, and the prevention of an arms race in outer space. The four intensive sessions produced some principles regarding a phased elimination of all nuclear weapons during a 10-year period. Previous differences were narrowed on such issues as intermediate-range nuclear forces (INF), testing, deep cuts in offensive nuclear missiles and their types.

Quite recently, however, NATO defense ministers met at Stavanger, Norway, and prompted a shift in the United States bargaining position in Geneva by which the remaining 200 INF warheads would be included in a prospective arms accord in line with President Reagan's desire for the

---

*Tunde Adeniran is professor of political science at the University of Ibadan, Nigeria.

elimination of all warheads. Apparently in reaction to this, during a Kremlin banquet in honor of visiting Vietnamese leader Nguyen Van Linh, General Secretary Gorbachev reiterated that the Soviet Union would resolve the problem of INF on a global basis if the United States agreed to dismantle its nuclear capability in Japan, the Republic of Korea, and the Philippines, as well as withdraw its aircraft carriers beyond agreed limits. All these, against the background of the superpowers' traditional postures and manipulations in the nuclear arms race, call for a critical examination of Reykjavik and beyond in our campaign for world disarmament.

The Antecedents

Since the beginning of the SALT negotiations in 1969, indeed since Stalin's death, Soviet-American relations have witnessed some ups and downs. It has been a long period of mutual frustrations and worrisome coexistence, the result of the strategic arms race and its action-reaction structure that sustains the inconclusiveness of the arms control negotiations. These negotiations should not be seen as mere processes and products of the arms competition between the United States and the Soviet Union; they lie at the center of world peace and international security.

For any analysis of the arms control negotiations to be relevant with respect to the present strategic situation and possible future trends, however, cognizance must be taken of their precedents. It is logical to trace their roots to the system of naval arms control established by the Washington Treaty Limiting Naval Armament of 1922 and the London Treaty for the Limitation and Reduction of Naval Armament of 1930 and the Protocol of 1936. These negotiations could be said to represent organized attempts to limit naval armaments in the interwar years in the same way in which SALT, the Strategic Arms Reduction Talks (START), and INF represent contemporary efforts to limit strategic armaments. With regard to SALT, for instance, this view is partly based on the premise identified by Hedley Bull as follows:

> First, the naval treaties were the result of realistic and businesslike negotiations designed to establish formal limitations on a particular category of armaments of major strategic importance . . . Second, the naval treaties were concerned with quantitative limitations . . . Third, in attempting to deal with 'the problem of the ratio' the naval arms negotiators accorded a central place to the idea of "parity" . . . Fourth, the naval treaties were an attempt

to determine an agreed ratio of naval strength among the dominant naval powers, especially the British Empire and the United States . . . Fifth, like SALT, the attempt to limit naval arms was part of a wider long-term disarmament effort . . . Sixth, in the naval arms conferences as in SALT, the discussions assumed that verification of any agreement would not require formal inspection procedures, "reciprocal" or international, but would be carried out by unilateral intelligence . . . [3]

The similarities between SALT and the naval treaties noted above are, without doubt, startling, but it is inaccurate to suggest that they alone constitute SALT's precedents. The historical basis of SALT could also be found in other negotiations whose format and subject were, of course, not very similar to those of SALT. The various proposals put forward between 1946 and 1960 for comprehensive disarmament were more ambitious than those contained in the SALT negotiations, whereas the latter—by emphasizing numerical limitation in addition to some prohibition—are of greater strategic significance than the nonproliferation treaty, the partial test ban treaty, and the outer space treaty. Yet all these treaties constitute the background to SALT, INF, START, and the Reykjavik meeting.

One factor that influenced the postglobal war, pre-SALT negotiations was the transformation of the global political situation. Not only did states terminate their obligations and violate specific disarmament provisions, but a chain of internal and external events was sparked off that altered the political and strategic context of any future superpower negotiations. Moreover, the possibility of greater technological innovation or breakthrough by an adversary prompted each superpower to wish to stabilize the strategic balance. Strategic calculations soon became compounded by economic, political, and technological rationales.[4]

The increase in defense expenditures that became apparent in the pre-SALT period was an indication that at some point it might become difficult for the two economic systems to sustain the strategic buildup. Politically, the opposing blocs had become relatively tolerant of each other toward the end of the 1960s and the possibility that the cold war would lead to a real or "hot" war by the superpowers was low. Added to this was the movement to settle the German question. But by far the most significant of the historical conditions or causal factors responsible for the SALT negotiations were (1) the rough parity between Soviet-American strategic nuclear forces and (2) widespread restiveness among the scientific elite, its pressure on the various governments' leadership,[5] and the latter's interest in preventing nuclear war.

The Ramifications of SALT

If negotiations have been based on the premises noted above, what then do they actually represent in a nuclear environment that is no longer bipolar? What are the objectives and their implications? We shall begin with SALT. Mason Willrich once noted that "the central meaning of SALT is political. In an overall appraisal of SALT, an enormous array of diverse military, economic, technical, and psychological factors must be filtered through a political lens. In so doing, the light from each factor is diffused and the images become blurred, but the impression one gains is closer to reality."[6]

SALT could also be interpreted to mean that the Soviet Union and the United States had heeded Sir Winston Churchill's advice that "jaw-jaw is better than war-war." SALT treaties have, of course, been part of the efforts to avoid war. We hardly need to be reminded that they were geared toward agreement on measures designed to limit strategic offensive forces, constrain strategic defensive systems, freeze qualitative improvements in weaponry, and curb the deployment of new weapons. The implications of these a decade ago were different for both the Soviet Union and the United States. The latter, for instance, had for almost two decades boasted of maintaining superior nuclear forces in terms of size, delivery capabilities, and flexibility of response.

In order for the superpowers to effectively limit their strategic offensive forces, they had to agree on the nature or categories of such forces, the level to set as the limit, and the extent and type (e.g., two-thirds of the existing submarine-launched ballistic missiles, bombers, etc.) of the limits. For them to constrain the strategic defenses, they had to ascertain *all* the uses to which the complex systems (including such equipment as the relatively simple fighter-interceptors) could be put and to be sure that agreed restrictions would be readily enforceable and easily verifiable. The freezing of qualitative improvements suggested preventing the production of larger missiles with heavier payloads[7] and perhaps limiting the accuracy of re-entry vehicles with the massive power to knock out land-based missiles. Finally, for any restriction on new weapons to be meaningful, the negotiating powers had to be in a position to regulate the development of new weapons (with attendant psychological and political advantages) capable of threatening the strategic balance and to forestall "cheating" in the game.

The above conditions were the major challenges faced by the two superpowers while negotiating the SALT I agreement in 1969—20 years

after the Soviet Union had shocked the United States by exploding a nuclear weapon and about a dozen years after the launching of Sputnik. But
for the Soviet invasion of Czechoslovakia in 1968, the talks might have
taken off then. That invasion was often cited as the reason for the U.S. review of its strategic options, and it was after the review had recom-
mended that the United States should settle for strategic parity that
President Nixon opted for a strategy of "nuclear sufficiency." Even then it
was difficult to resolve the problem of emphasis in strategic policy, that
is, whether it should be on bombers or missiles, offense or defense, intercontinental ballistic missile (ICBM) or submarine-launched ballistic missile (SLBM), etc.

The entire process of SALT was geared toward stability, which could be
viewed as twofold or manifold. It was, indeed, concerned essentially with
crisis stability and dynamic stability. Of course, SALT I started a process
of mutual enlightenment, which was necessary for achieving its ultimate
goal of preventing any strategic nuclear war, and was dictated by the logic
of national security. The first phase of the negotiations, SALT I, brought
about the signing of two agreements: the first, the Treaty limiting ABM
systems, and the second, the Interim Agreement providing for certain
limitations on strategic offensive weapons for a five-year period. Both entered into force on 3 October 1972.

SALT II, the second phase of the bilateral negotiations, started in November 1972 and continued for two years, leading to a joint statement on
24 November 1974 at Vladivostok, USSR. There and then the U.S. President and the General Secretary of the Communist Party of the Soviet
Union agreed, in principle, that a new agreement should be concluded in
1975 to cover the period until 31 December 1985. The general provisions
of the agreement were to include limiting the aggregate number of strategic delivery vehicles on each side to 2,400 and establishing a sublimit of
1,320 on ICBMs and SLBMs equipped with multiple independently targetable re-entry vehicles (MIRVs).

Since SALT I was able to achieve so much, greater expectation was
placed on SALT II. For instance, SALT I's ABM Treaty was able to limit
ABM systems to only one site for each side (the two originally permitted
under the Treaty were reduced to one by the ABM Protocol of July 1974)
for ABM deployment—with tight restrictions on the ABM launchers and
radars at the site. The Interim Agreement on strategic offensive arms and
its Protocol froze the number of fixed ICBM launchers and permitted an
increase in SLBM launchers up to an agreed level. Thus the United States
was allowed 1,054 ICBMs and 710 SLBM launchers, and the Soviet

Union was allowed 1,618 ICBMs and 950 SLBMs. There was speculation that the United States was compensated for the Soviet Union's numerical advantage by some brand of heavy bombers and MIRVs. With this achievement by SALT I, why did SALT II—among other goals—ascertain numerical equivalence?

With the deployment of a new set of high-payload ICBMs (the SS-17, 18, and 19) tested with MIRVs by the Soviet Union in late 1973, the American leadership was faced with the challenge of forcing the Soviet Union to limit the total payload or throw-weight that its missile force could deliver, but President Nixon's attempt at this did not succeed. This, at least, could be said to partially explain why the Ford administration, during the November 1974 negotiations at Vladivostok, returned to the simpler and less controversial principle of only limiting launcher numbers in a new treaty lasting until 1985. It was possible to eventually adopt the equal ceilings for three reasons:

1. The ceiling would not compel the Soviet Union to undertake any reductions in its growing arsenal and would, of course, include heavy bombers in which the United States had a crucial edge.
2. The American leadership was convinced that the ceilings would not deter it from responding to any Soviet buildup either by deploying a larger proportion of forces at sea or by replacing the Minuteman ICBM forces with a new mobile missile (such as the American air force's all-powerful 150,000-lb MX, which had not gone beyond the stage of proposition).
3. The Soviet aircraft bomber TU-26, known as "Backfire" in NATO circles, was not brought under the 2,250 ceiling on overall launchers. In the opinion of the Soviet Union, the TU-26 was an intermediate-range system, deployed primarily for use against targets in Western Europe and East Asia. This argument placed the Soviet bomber on the same plane as the American cruise missile.

The negotiators on both sides were, of course, aware that the TU-26 was indeed a medium-range bomber. But they were also aware that it could acquire a genuine two-way intercontinental capability with aerial refueling. Like the cruise missile, it was left out of the ceiling because its production rate would be frozen and its basing, refueling, and modernization would be restricted. Other relevant provisions of the SALT II Treaty included a ceiling of 1,320 (within the 2,250 aggregate) on the total number of land and sea-based MIRVed missiles, as well as heavy bombers equipped with air-launched cruise missiles (ALCMs); a subceiling of 1,200 on the total number of land and sea-based MIRVed missiles and an 820 subceiling on MIRVed ICBMs. Moreover, new missiles with payloads exceeding the Soviet SS-19 ("Savage's Uncle") would be counted as heavy ICBMs, whereas the testing and deployment of long-range ALCMs were to be restricted to such heavy bombers as the Soviet Bear and Bison aircraft and the American B-52s.

Provisions were also made in the Treaty to limit the range of ALCMs deployed aboard heavy bombers to 2,500 km and to prohibit both the rapid reloading of ICBM silos and the storage of excess missiles at launching sites. To ensure compliance, the two parties were prohibited from transferring the weapons limited in the Treaty to third parties and were required to provide each other with necessary information regarding missile testing as well as the size and performance of their respective arsenals. They were also, of course, to desist from interfering with the national technical means of verification provided for in the Treaty.

It can be seen from the above historical outline that the SALT II ceilings were rather high. But whereas the restrictions on qualitative improvements on weapons were inadequate and the Treaty did not fully take care of verification problems, it did—at least—allow some parity in numbers and reduced the chances of either side's acquiring first-strike capability. Moreover, apart from the Protocol, designed to codify the restrictions on weapons modernization, SALT II's Joint Statement of Principles provided a framework for future negotiations.

It was generally thought that the next round of talks would be SALT III and that they would focus on Western Europe and on reductions in forces. For instance, the Soviet Union was reportedly already "pushing for recognition of the concept that American nuclear-capable aircraft in Western Europe (so-called forward-based systems, or FES) and allied strategic nuclear forces (the British and French SLBMs forces) be subject to limitation in a future agreement,"[8] whereas the Americans would want new qualitative limits in terms of research and development in addition to reductions in forces. Future negotiations could be anticipated to entail a discussion of the cruise missiles and the TU-26 as well as the British and French nuclear forces. The relatively new Soviet SS-20 issue would be raised and so would the entire NATO-Warsaw Treaty nuclear balance. The Soviet Union, however, was not likely to be forced to negotiate under the threat of possible American deployment of MX ICBM in any mode.

START, INF, and Recurrent Problems of the Arms Control Negotiations

The United States failed to ratify a number of arms accords signed between 1974 and 1979. Today, some of the observations we made exactly one decade ago are still valid with regard to the problems involved in negotiating those agreements.[9] The existing and recurring problems are all related to the pattern of negotiation and its underlying factors. These factors include the issue at stake and the procedure for carrying out any decisions reached in the negotiations.

SALT eventually gave way to the START and INF talks, which collapsed in 1983. At the talks, the United States considered strategic buildup and the deployment of Pershing II and cruise missiles in Europe. In spite of the Soviet Union's awareness of the sophistication of these systems, especially with regard to short warning time and unpredictable trajectory, the proposal put forth by the Kremlin's delegation did not go beyond requesting that the United States forego the submarine-launched cruise missiles (SLCMs). The Soviet Union was, of course, also interested in equal cuts rather than deep asymmetrical reductions in the relevant systems. And it was worried about the anticipated militarization of space. Whereas planning its own space-based systems and improving existing offensive arms and other strategic defense, the Soviet Union started raising objections to SDI, proposed by Reagan on 23 March 1983 as a comprehensive defense or "shield" to render strategic nuclear weapons obsolete. Indeed, the fear of "Star Wars" might have induced the Geneva agreement between Secretary of State George Shultz and Foreign Minister Andrei Gromyko. But the shadow boxing continued and the circle of negotiations was later to be retraced.

The recurring problems of the arms control negotiations therefore derive from the American leadership's military-political thought and from Soviet official military-strategic planning. For both, nuclear weapons have become legal instruments for policy implementation—and this strategic posture of the two sides has become compounded by the problem of perception. For quite some time, many pressure groups in the United States have viewed the Soviet Union as seeking strategic superiority and the capacity to destroy American strategic retaliatory capacity through a pre-emptive or disarming first strike. To some, the appropriate response to this would be for the United States to improve its counterforce capabilities and develop mobile or multiple aim-point, land-based missiles. Some reason that the United States might, in fact, need to deter the

Soviet Union by ensuring stability through strategic force invulnerability, whereas others call for the production of far more sophisticated weapons, unknown before, so as to put an end to Soviet ambition to become a global military power second to none.

Some members of the American Congress often regard any concessions in the negotiations as disastrous. For instance, they considered SALT II as leaving the mainstay of the American land-based nuclear deterrent— the Minuteman ICBMs—vulnerable by the early 1980s to virtual destruction on a first strike delivered by a fraction of the total Soviet missile force. It was also believed that the agreement would limit (1) the range of all cruise missiles (which, with the MX missile, represented the bargaining chip referred to sometimes as "the missile the Russians fear most") and (2) the number of long-range manned bombers, while ensuring that the Soviet Union would have at least twice as many ICBM warheads as the United States.[10]

Moreover, the political forces within the United States that view the country as being short-changed through the arms control negotiations stressed that American land-based ICBMs would be vulnerable, and that SALT II would permit the development of Soviet air-defense systems, which could blunt the effectiveness of the American bomber force, making the capacity for assured retaliation more heavily dependent on submarine-based missiles. But a far more fundamental American perception was the feeling that American negotiators were being too eager to please and that the United States could soon be led into a position of strategic inferiority. And there were also those who believed (and many still do) that American participation in the negotiations had been predicated on the assumption that any treaty should stabilize the international strategic balance without placing the United States in an inferior position to the Soviet Union, and that it should allow the United States to maintain an intensive research, development, and weapon-modernization program. In their eyes, the SALT II Treaty did not meet any of these requirements.

Apart from the mutual accusation of reacting negatively to proposals rather than showing initiative by offering proposals, the Soviet Union, too, has its own unpleasant views of the negotiations. It is often irritated by some American leaders' public styles, which frequently cast the United States in the role of innovator and initiator while portraying the Soviet Union as obstructing the arms negotiations.

Moreover, the Soviet side suspects and is doubtful about most moves made by the United States. For instance, it was the United States that introduced the MIRVs to destabilize existing weapons and planned the deployment of long-range cruise missiles for greater destabilization of the system. Other Soviet resentments during the mid-1970s revolved around the American proposal for substantial reductions in deployment of land-based ICBMs—part of the backbone of Soviet military strength—including cutting by as much as 50 percent their largest missiles already in place, and the fact that this proposal made no provision for reducing or restraining systems in which the United States had an advantage, such as the Trident submarine or the B-1 bomber. Moreover, the limitation proposed for cruise missiles was grossly inadequate from the Soviet perspective.

And so the problems became wider in scope. They went beyond issues relating to mutual suspicion, such as the problem of reconciling common ceilings and reductions. One of these problems was the so-called gray area issue or the dual-capable systems. These figure both in the direct United States-Soviet strategic relationship and in any assessment of balance in the European theatre. They include the U.S. cruise missiles and forward-based aircraft in Europe and the Soviet Union's Backfire bomber and some intermediate-range missiles like the SS-20. The problem here has been the significant disagreement over the definition of the mission of the weapons and whether or not to include them in the list that had, in the past, been limited to those capable of reaching the other side's homeland. Today there is a new bargaining chip. SDI, designed to create either a space shield or insurance against retaliation for a nuclear first strike by the United States against the Soviet Union, has added its own complications.

Before the United States sought new leverage through SDI, an earlier expectation was that the negotiations would cover issues with which such forums as the Conference on Security and Co-operation in Europe (CSCE) were preoccupied. These include nuclear test bans and the search for parity of strength through symmetric reductions, the latter being advocated in the name of mutual and balanced force reductions. Whereas any reduction to a common ceiling would mean greater reduction on the part of the Warsaw Treaty, it was still felt in some quarters in the United States that such agreements with the Treaty could restrict NATO's future options, whereas, from the Soviet viewpoint, there would be political instability in Europe unless some rational restrictions were placed on Western military options. These suspicions and fears no doubt derive from some structural deficiencies in the two organizations, but they have become important factors in their perception of the strategic balance.

There is, finally, a recurrent problem of violations and inadequate means of verification. There have been allegations and counterallegations of cheating. Each side claims that the other is (1) engaged in illegal construction of new weapons, (2) testing and concealing some weapon systems in violation of certain articles of the SALT agreement, and (3) blinding, i.e., obstructing, the photographing or monitoring of new weapons. All these contravene the commitment of both sides to noninterference with each other's independent means of verification, the national technical means of verification that were to be used in a manner consistent with generally recognized principles of international law. And, because these means include the blockable satellite-based sensors of various types used to monitor each other's compliance, ELINT (electronic intelligence) and other intelligence collection techniques and technologies whose processes could be impaired, there are many grounds for mutual suspicion. There has, therefore, been an urgent need for means that could not be easily intercepted. The danger of disinformation does not make the problem less complex—in spite of the SALT II Common Understanding not to impede verification through encryption of signals from missiles being tested as well as the recent agreement to go beyond national means of verification.

Moreover, the basic goal of the negotiations has been to ensure a reduction in the existing levels of nuclear weapons and to restrain the introduction of new systems so that the strategic balance is not destabilized. This goal cannot be attained without compliance and this, too, can only be ascertained through both national and nonnational technical means of verification. With regard to the nonnational means, each side is not likely to allow more than a few visits to test sites and selected installations. And, as has been observed, the existing national technical means are "vulnerable to measures that may *degrade* their assumed effectiveness, *interrupt* their functioning, or *prevent* their operation."[11] What then could sustain the negotiations and guarantee compliance with negotiated agreements? A logical answer would be to introduce the use of aircraft reconnaisance—since it would neither encounter any natural inhibitions (such as bad weather or darkness) nor follow a path and schedule in such a way that major weapons activity or strategic gadgetry could be concealed from it. This means (as part of the nonnational) would not, of course, be acceptable for political reasons, and so the agreements could be abandoned.

The negotiations have therefore continued to afford the powers the opportunity to play the strategic game as if it were chess or backgammon. They have at the back of their minds the desire for armed strength to contain or deter the other. Their ultimate objective, however, is to win the game or strike a balance or draw, if winning becomes impossible. Winning, in this case, implies strengthening or enhancing one's strategic position relative to the opponent's, whereas a draw means leaving the relative positions substantially unaltered. Willingness to play the game (negotiate) is generated by some compulsion.

Another look at the salient issues involved in the negotiations would confirm the points above. For instance, "strategic parity" has become almost a creed. Whereas MIRV deployment might not be affected, numerical parity would allow the United States to build an ABM system approximately as big as that around Moscow while the Soviet Union could increase its submarine missile force several times over. This development could lead—on either side—to such an expansion of long-range bomber forces (with newer aircraft) that the essence of parity could be nullified. Each side is aware that effective negotiations require rough parity of forces. One implication of this is that the European balance (both nuclear and conventional) should not be handled within the context of the Vienna Talks on Mutual Reduction of Forces and Armaments and Associated Measures in Central Europe, which cover only the central front. Instead, the superpowers should ensure that it is taken up by a new group comprising the 35 signatories of the 1975 Final Act of the CSCE. This would allow greater attention to be focused on the area stretching from the Atlantic to the Urals in the discussions on nuclear overkill.

Bureaucratic politics or technological imperatives have also introduced some factors into the negotiations. The bargaining chip is one such factor, and it can hardly enhance trust or be effectively kept clear of projected force postures. Let us take the ABM Treaty, for instance. It is a classic example of a bargaining chip. It's not wanted and not needed, but one negotiator thinks he must have it so that he can give it away in exchange for another bargaining chip, which the other did not want and did not need but acquired for the same purpose. Before Reykjavik, the blackmail revolved around the militarization of space. The situation now seems to have altered slightly.

Moreover, the environment of the negotiations also tends to compound the problem. Both sides have domestic constituencies with their peculiar problems. To sell any agreements to these constituencies they have to convince them that the men on the other side are reliable negotiating partners and that they themselves can remain tough.

The superpowers demonstrate adequate awareness of the need to restrain the strategic arms competition, but they are not prepared to suppress threatening technical developments or prevent the dangerous qualitative improvements in strategic forces. They tend to prolong the negotiations through piecemeal measures, if only because they want to prevent a return to the cold war or are, in fact, not sure of the true status of their relative capabilities.

In spite of the "progress" made after many years of negotiating agreements and some co-operation in areas where there is continuing risk of inadvertent conflict,[12] the two sides really do not have the full facts before them to guarantee meaningful and permanent agreements and there is no law to ensure that they will get them. For instance, despite United States claims that the Soviet Union got more than it did from SALT II, did the United States make any distinction between the Minuteman II (which carries a single nuclear warhead) and the Minuteman III (which can carry three MIRVs)? And is the Soviet Union sure how many warheads would be put on the Minuteman III? Yet there was the common fear in the West that its ability to deter Soviet attack was failing at all levels—conventional, theater nuclear, and strategic. The United States consequently launched the MX missile in California in June 1985. The Soviet Union was not, however, going to remain idle until the formal deployment of the American MX force, which, with its 200 missile and 2,000 warheads, was expected to be able to destroy all the Soviet Union's land-based missiles in a first strike. In other words, technical advances in weaponry and the possible inclusion of some new issues and parties are seen as likely to further complicate the problem of classification at the negotiations. This is all the more likely since a Soviet general and an American general do not see the military situation the same way and are not likely to agree on what is equitable. But Reykjavik has, at last, added a new dimension.

Reykjavik's Zero-Zero Option

Reykjavik has come as an unusual, but timely, development. So much hope had been placed on the Geneva summit of 1985, which produced so little. Indeed, apart from the symbolism of the summit and the pointer it gave to the future, there was nothing else that was reassuring about the future of arms limitation and disarmament. There was, of course, an American-sponsored resolution in the First Committee of the General Assembly calling on all States to recognize the overriding importance of compliance with arms limitation and disarmament agreements, which was adopted without a negative vote. The resolution recognized the fact that any violation of compliance with arms control agreements affects both the security of States party to them and that of other States relying on constraints and commitments stipulated in the agreements. But the resolution could only call on the countries that have signed disarmament agreements to fully live up to their provisions and could not compel the Soviet Union and the United States to continue talking at the bilateral summit until the arms control issues on their agenda were resolved. Yet the achievements of the two superpowers in this regard would dictate the course and consequence of the arms race. And this is why Reykjavik roused such great hopes.

The policy reformulations and initiatives that one has observed in Gorbachev's administration seem to have been carried to Reykjavik. There we saw a recast of Soviet positions on INFs—a far cry from the November 1983 episode—a new Soviet perspective on the Atlantic alliance and an overall commitment to make concessions. Back in January 1986, Gorbachev had launched some comprehensive proposals that included the complete elimination of nuclear weapons by the year 2000. This was to be followed by the removal of tactical and short-range missiles. And, because of the Americans' constant desire to establish linkage between their perception of Soviet strength in land-based nuclear weapons and the usefulness of the United States SDI in the offense-defense equation, Gorbachev had (at the June 1986 meeting of the Political Consultative Committee of the Warsaw Treaty in Budapest) proposed that the negotiating zone be from the Atlantic to the Urals, phased troop reductions (of 100,000–150,000 troops within two years and up to 500,000 soldiers and airmen by the early 1990s) and cuts in tactical nuclear aircraft and nuclear weapons with ranges of over 1,000 kilometers.

The foregoing were reflected in Reykjavik, where General Secretary Gorbachev appeared quite ready to accept substantial cuts in Soviet missile forces in exchange for American agreement to abide by the ABM Treaty for 10 years and confine SDI research to the laboratory. In President Reagan's view, the United States would need SDI to provide a defensive shield against any offensive nuclear forces—some deterrence more or less in the tradition of "mutual assured destruction" (MAD).

At the end of the Reykjavik summit, the superpowers agreed to halve strategic offensive weapons during the first five years of a 10-year period. They also agreed on a reduction to 100 warheads on medium-range missiles in both the Asian part of the USSR and the United States own territory, zero medium-range missiles for both sides in Europe, and a freeze on the existing number of short-range missiles deployed there.

In short, the Americans had less cause to worry much about the long-dreaded SS-18s (with their accuracy, speed, and destructive capacity) and other large Soviet multiple-warhead ICBMs. Efforts were also made to restrict both sides to weapons that lack first-strike capability—cruise missiles, bombers, and the small single-warhead mobile ICBMs that are designed essentially for retaliation. Whereas something has been gained at Reykjavik, the problem remains how to fully reconcile the American desire for reduction in what they classify as offensive forces with the Soviet interest in restraining such high-technology means of destruction as space strike arms (which the Americans see as part of their defensive systems).

For now, at least, the superpowers have agreed to some form of zero option, which means withdrawal of the intermediate-range missiles that threaten Europe. The proposal to ban all ballistic missiles within 10 years could also help the cause of arms control and the search for global peace through disarmament. But the two leaders need to be faithful to the spirit of the negotiations and also work hard to convince powerful groups within their national and global constituencies. With improved relations with China (the cultural and economic agreements signed during the past two years should pave the way) and some flexibility toward Japan and the West, it would be possible to allay the fears (especially in Britain and France) that any Soviet-American nuclear deal could become devastating to Western Europe's nuclear deterrents. Whereas antinuclear sentiment is running deep into the heart of Europe, official promoters of strategic linkage are also at work, lobbying against any "comprehensive compromise" that would promote peace but threaten their purse. This is why the world has been witnessing conflicting interpretations of Reykjavik, especially at official levels, as in the November 1986 discussions on arms control between American Secretary of State Shultz and Soviet Foreign Minister Shevardnadze and in the nuclear and space talks in Geneva.

Future success will depend on a number of factors. The arms control negotiations have usually been viewed simply as the continuing negotiations between the United States and the Soviet Union on the issue of limiting and reducing strategic nuclear weapons. But the negotiations are broader than this in terms of scope and implications. The proximate goal is, of course, the stabilization of the relationship of mutual nuclear deterrence between the superpowers. But the broader implications suggest:

1. The possibility of antagonistic states collaborating on the control of nuclear weapons.
2. The likelihood of achieving a demilitarized international society in which nuclear war would become less likely.

3. The probability of halting nuclear proliferation, vertically and horizontally.
4. The practicability of formally reducing the risk of nuclear war through specific treaties.

The points noted above suggest that whereas the arms control negotiations could promote objectives that are primarily bilateral, they have universal implications as well. Their purposes are indeed universal in that they entail reductions in the arsenals for killing or maiming people who are not necessarily Soviet or American citizens. They have also been motivated by certain political and economic reasons, whose essence and spillover effects bear upon the structure of the international system. Indeed, the potential of the negotiations goes beyond merely restricting the competition between the two nuclear superpowers and setting a limit to the superiority they have over other nations. The negotiations are based in part on the prevailing strategic situation of the international system and on—in the words of the preamble of the ABM Treaty—"the premise that nuclear war would have devastating consequences for all mankind." The nature of the negotiations as international phenomena requiring international agreement is reinforced by the realization that seeking an end to vertical proliferation by the superpowers is a necessary condition for halting horizontal proliferation among the potential nuclear powers.

On the whole, the history, patterns, and problems of the arms control negotiations attest to the fact that the two superpowers and the rest of the world—especially Europe—which constantly hinder rather than help the talks with their strategic policies are to blame for the lack of decision to move toward a complete ban on the production of nuclear weapons and their elimination. This is the dilemma before us and it must be faced squarely. Negotiations remain the principal means of resolving the inherent and recurring problems, but their success depends on the goodwill and political will of the parties involved. There is need for compliance with the principle of equal security and a genuine appreciation of the nuclear danger to the world. The march toward arms limitation and global disarmament and a meaningful halt to the nuclear arms race can therefore be achieved only through increased pressures by international governmental and nongovernmental organizations as well as national groups and associations, and with the participation of all nuclear powers (and some nonnuclear weapon states as Observers) in negotiations on ending the production of nuclear weapons and on eliminating their stockpiles.

Notes

1. See the recent issue of Richard Hudson's Center for War/Peace Studies *Newsletter* (New York: 1987).

2. Klaus Knorr, "Controlling nuclear war," *International Security*, 9, No. 4 (spring 1985), 79.

3. Hedley Bull, "Strategic arms limitation: The precedent of the Washington and London naval Treaties," Norton A. Kaplan, ed., *SALT: Problems and Prospects* (Morristown, NJ: General Learning Press, 1973), pp. 26–30.

4. For a detailed analysis of these rationales and other relevant factors, see J. I. Coffey, *Strategic Power and National Security* (Pittsburgh: University of Pittsburgh Press, 1971).

5. The popular assumption in the West is that, unlike in the United States, dissent in the Soviet Union is often muffled and it would be impossible for any pressure group to make the Soviet leadership change a policy position. In the case of SALT, Andrei Sakharov and others did succeed in influencing the Soviet leadership on the antiballistic missile issue. Chernenko appeared more vulnerable to pressures than any of his predecessors, whereas Gorbachev has signaled his flexibility.

6. Mason Willrich, "SALT I: An Appraisal," Mason Willrich and Bohn B. Rhinelander, eds., *SALT: The Moscow Agreements and Beyond* (New York: The Free Press, 1974), p. 256.

7. Only a few of these are needed to wipe out civilian populations. The possessor is therefore at a great advantage regarding high-yield warheads for effective counterforce attacks.

8. See Richard Burt, "The scope and limits of SALT," *Foreign Affairs*, July 1978, pp. 759–760.

9. See Tunde Adeniran, "Africa and the strategic arms limitation talks," *AFRICA*, No. 70, June 1977.

10. See Representative Charles H. Wilson's "SALT II—blueprint for disaster," *The Reader's Digest* (April 1978), pp. 89–92.

11. Robert Perry, "Verifying SALT in the 1980s," Christoph Bertram, ed., *The Future of Arms Control: Part I—Beyond SALT II*, Adelphi Paper No. 141, spring 1978, p. 18.

12. For a comprehensive analysis of this, see Michael M. May, "The U.S.-Soviet Approach to Nuclear Weapons," *International Security*, 9, No. 4 (spring 1985), 140–153.

REYKJAVIK AND PROSPECTS FOR
A NUCLEAR-FREE WORLD

*Aleksandr A. Bessmertnykh**

Political analysts, diplomats, and politicians have come to regard as natural the linkage between Reykjavik and prospects for a radical reduction in nuclear arms.

The meeting in the Icelandic capital marked a turning-point in the search for a conceptual approach to and a practical solution of the crucial problem of today, namely, the elimination of nuclear arms. The meeting owes its significance primarily to the fact that the leaders of the two powers possessing the world's largest nuclear arsenals discussed in concrete terms the ways to implement deep cuts in their arsenals and almost succeeded in elaborating a diplomatic formula that could produce agreement.

In this respect, Reykjavik was no accident. In fact, it crowned the long-standing efforts of those who advocate solution of the problem of nuclear overarmament—initially through reducing the nuclear capabilities of the Soviet Union and the United States. The intellectual breakthrough in Reykjavik reflected the awareness—at least on the Soviet side—that a higher level of nuclear confrontation could at some point diminish military-strategic stability instead of enhancing it, even if parity were strictly maintained.

For that key conclusion to be made, we had to review analytically the traditional approaches to and established notions about peace and security. In other words, we had to apply new thinking to the major issue of our times. In the process of sorting out outdated dogmas and stereotypes, we arrived at two fundamental conclusions. First, in terms of the supreme interests of survival, the world is one, notwithstanding its diversity. Compared to all other class, bloc, or national interests, the task of preventing nuclear war holds absolute primacy. Second, the security of any State would be greater if it abandoned attempts to diminish the security of the other side. In other words, in terms of the Soviet-United States relationship, the Soviet Union has no interest in seeing U.S. security diminished,

---

*Aleksandr A. Bessmertnykh is Deputy Minister of Foreign Affairs of the USSR.

as this would stimulate a dangerous arms race and lead to dangerous instability.

Unfortunately, however, many people in the West tend to regard such a decisive turnabout in the established approach as heresy, inconsistent with the way of thinking that is generally accepted, not because of its inherent logic, but only because it has been so long and so blindly held in awe. Apparently this is also due to the fact that progress in physics and military technology has overtaken progress in political thinking.

In practical terms, Reykjavik continues to exert an effect in that the ongoing talks on strategic offensive arms, medium-range missiles, and the strengthening of the antiballistic missile (ABM) Treaty régime (which the two sides agreed not to withdraw from for at least 10 years) are proceeding on the basis of agreements and understandings reached there between the leaders of the Soviet Union and the United States, despite remaining differences. The USSR does not retreat from the parameters discussed there and is ready to travel its part of the road toward the implementation of what was discussed in Reykjavik.

Obstacles

What are the difficulties standing in the way of treaties and agreements on nuclear disarmament?

First, as Mikhail Gorbachev recently noted, the main obstacles are of a political nature. This is a matter of political will, a matter of intentions.

Second, military and political concepts and doctrines of the 1940s and 1950s prevail in the West. They are built either on the misconceptions arising from the West's short-lived nuclear monopoly and nuclear-missile superiority or on a deification of nuclear weapons as supernatural peacekeepers. The doctrine of flexible response is nothing but a camouflage for claiming a right to deliver a first nuclear strike. A potential explosion is inherent in the concept of nuclear deterrence, a concept that is being ripped apart by internal contradictions. One cannot say that a nuclear conflict would be a catastrophe for all of us and argue a moment later that nuclear weapons should be retained as a means of preserving peace.

Third, it is the persistent desire of some of our negotiating partners to strengthen their security at the expense of others rather than together with them. Hence, endless tactical fuss and attempts to drown agreement in linkages and reservations and to gain unilateral advantages.

Fourth, there are efforts to ensure security by military and technological, rather than political, means, that is, through pursuing the arms race and opening up new channels for it. A concentrated expression of these attempts today is the SDI program.

Fifth, there are the obstacles of a psychological nature that manifest themselves first and foremost in cultivating an image of other peoples as the enemy, in exaggerating the differences in states' political systems and policies, and so on. Moreover, weapons and fear and weapons and mistrust are communicating vessels that feed each other.

In these circumstances a logical question arises: Is the Soviet Union's goal of building a nuclear-free world realistic at all? We answer this question in the affirmative.

People tend to view ideas that are in advance of contemporary thinking as Utopian. However, if experts could study closely the program of a nuclear-free world formulated in detail by Mikhail Gorbachev in his statement of 15 January 1986, they would see for themselves that this program is fair and pragmatic in every aspect. If the United States or other countries desire to make a contribution of their own to the further development of this program, they are welcome to do so.

What proves the feasibility of plans to drastically cut nuclear arms and later, at a certain stage, to eliminate them? Laying no claims to give an exhaustive answer, I would mention several factors that, in our view, prove that the nuclear disarmament program is feasible.

1. The nature of proposals to this effect advanced by the Soviet Union are specific and balanced in character. The phased implementation of reductions deserves special mention. The concept of a phased approach incorporates the principle of maintaining stability and balance at progressively lower levels of confrontation. This is true of our proposals on strategic offensive arms, medium-range missiles, and nuclear explosions.
2. Great progress has been made in dealing with the issue of verification of the reduction and elimination of nuclear weapons. One can say today that the number of points of convergence on this key element of the process of real disarmament has increased significantly. A solid basis for productive negotiations exists.
3. An entire system of confidence-building measures is already in operation in Europe and has been further elaborated for other regions, in particular for Asia. The decisions taken at Stockholm have contributed to progress in the field of disarmament.
4. The very size of the arsenals that have been built up—about 25,000

nuclear weapons on strategic delivery vehicles alone—demonstrates
that overarmament has reached a level that argues convincingly in
favor of practical reduction.

5. Sufficient advance has been made in developing the theoretical and
conceptual basis of nuclear weapons reductions, in particular as an
essential element in strengthening strategic stability.

The USSR deems it advisable to approach the solution of security and
strategic stability problems on a wide front, covering—apart from nuclear arms—conventional and chemical weapons, the strengthening of
the régime of the treaties in force, and the prevention of an arms race in
space.

What measures can be taken in the short-term and medium-term perspective? A realistic possibility at present would be the elaboration of a
treaty on medium-range and operational-tactical missiles. The importance of such an agreement stems from the fact that it would rid Europe
of an entire class of nuclear missile systems. Furthermore, certain of its
aspects (e.g., verification provisions) could serve as a useful precedent for
working out subsequent agreements on the reduction of other types of nuclear arms. A medium-range missile treaty would be the first practical
and constructive step toward this goal.

The questions of reducing strategic offensive arms and preventing an
arms race in outer space are more complex. But in this case, too, we believe it will be quite possible to agree on the key provisions of future accords in the next few months. Naturally we are also prepared to conclude
complete treaties on these questions. As Mikhail Gorbachev has noted
recently, the most important task at this moment is to preserve the ABM
Treaty. Should the Treaty be violated, the negotiations would lose their
value, the arms race would get out of control, and suspicion and mistrust
would grow. If, on the other hand, the ABM Treaty is preserved and
strengthened, new vistas will open for rapid progress in the remaining
years of the decade and the 1990s toward a nuclear-free world.

What is our vision of a nuclear-free world? As early as the beginning of
the 1990s, we could rid Europe of both medium-range and operational-
tactical nuclear missiles. As to the nuclear systems still remaining there
and a limited number of nuclear warheads on medium-range missiles deployed in Asia and in U.S. territory, we feel that they should also be included in the agenda of subsequent negotiations. The problem of tactical
nuclear weapons would be addressed concurrently with armed forces and
conventional arms reductions.

While eliminating in Europe a dangerous concentration of nuclear arms deployed in the zone dividing the two politico-military alliances, the United States and the Soviet Union would also cut their strategic offensive arsenals by 50 percent within a five-year period, provided, of course, that the ABM Treaty remained in effect and that all attempts to break the existing structure of Soviet strategic potential were abandoned. Later on, agreement should be sought on a phased elimination of the remaining strategic offensive arms.

During the first stage in the process of radically reducing and eliminating nuclear arms, the two sides would gain some valuable experience in the application of procedures, principles, and mechanisms related to mutual verification, which, in turn, would serve as a factor ensuring security. The Soviet Union stands for the strictest possible verification, including inspections of facilities where missiles are to be dismantled and destroyed, test ranges and military bases, including those located in third countries, and plants and depots, both government-owned and private.

It would be extremely important to compare the military doctrines of NATO and of the Warsaw Treaty and to examine how they might evolve in the future. This would dispel mutual suspicion and distrust, while making military doctrines and concepts fundamentally defensive.

In accordance with the Soviet-proposed concept, all disarmament and confidence-building measures should lead in the long run to the establishment of a comprehensive security system in the political, economic, and humanitarian fields.

This is the multilayer structure we envisage that should serve as a basis of a nuclear-free world.

POSSIBILITIES AFTER REYKJAVIK: LET US NOT WASTE THEM

*Julio C. Carasales**

The subject of this meeting takes Reykjavik as a point of departure, and rightly so. Obviously, no miracles happened at Reykjavik. Miracles rarely happen at summit meetings. At the same time, what did happen at Reykjavik was not totally unexpected. The main themes had been around for years. It is also true that great discrepancies arose immediately after Reykjavik about what really happened there, about the exact degree and substance of the convergence of views that was on the brink of being achieved.

Notwithstanding all that, it has to be recognized that Reykjavik has come to be regarded, rightly or wrongly—and I think rightly—as the beginning of a new era in the arms control and disarmament field. It is seen as a breakthrough, as a hopeful sign that a world free of nuclear weapons need not always remain an illusion or a goal to which politicians pay lip service from time to time, without any realistic possibility of ever being attained or, at least, achieved in the foreseeable future.

The position of the Third World regarding nuclear weapons is too well known to require repetition here. Governments and peoples share a total rejection of those instruments of mass destruction. In the developed world, the situation is not the same. It is a fact that one of the two great military alliances bases its defense policy on nuclear deterrence, but, at the same time, I think it is also a fact that the great majority of the population of the West is completely against nuclear weapons. The other military alliance is on record as favoring a no-first-use policy, but nuclear weapons are an important part of its arsenal and it has been asserted that it practices, without officially saying so, a policy not very different from the one followed by its rival. In any case, the danger of a nuclear war is always present, and its consequences have been described too many times for the words "a nuclear war cannot be won and should never be fought" not to meet with universal approval.

---

*Julio César Carasales is Special Adviser to the Secretary of State for International Relations of Argentina.

It was somewhat distressing, therefore, at least from a Third World point of view, that the results or, to be exact, the possibilities opened at Reykjavik were received with reservations, sometimes with strong reservations, in certain circles. No treaties were signed at Reykjavik, nothing was really agreed to, but the mere possibility of making great advances toward the elimination of whole categories of nuclear weapons was enough to cause great concern, even in quarters not often associated with hardline attitudes or with distrust about arms control in general.

Some hoped, it seemed, that Reykjavik would just go away. The linkage between nuclear missiles and SDI made possible—fortunately, in their opinion—any agreement. World leaders were saved from their own thoughtlessness. Nuclear weapons and their means of delivery would remain untouched and would continue to be the guardians of peace and security.

But, unhappily for those who thought along those lines, Reykjavik did not fade away. What was discussed there were not just political maneuvers or propaganda tricks without real content. The Soviet Union has dropped the above-mentioned linkage related to SDI. Important reductions in the number of nuclear warheads and means of delivery seem to be underway. Long-range intermediate nuclear forces (INF) in Europe could be completely eliminated. Both sides agree to the zero option. Up to 100 missiles will remain in Asia and 100 in the United States, outside Europe. The short-range intermediate nuclear forces, regarding which one side is said to enjoy a 9-1 advantage, were also thrown into the package. They could disappear, too. A Europe free of nuclear weapons seems a goal that could realistically be achieved in the near future, not an illusory mirage.

Two major difficulties seem to face this grand design. One is natural and logical. Verification is an indispensable and fundamental component of any disarmament agreement—not just any kind of verification, but an efficient system of verification, to the satisfaction of both sides. One side should be reasonably sure that the other side does not cheat. The word "reasonably" should be underlined. A system 100 percent perfect just does not exist. To try to reach the unattainable is to deny the possibility of ever getting disarmament agreements. On the other hand, a country that has historically always been very reluctant to accept verification measures that it has considered "intrusive" seems now to be changing that attitude. The field is open, therefore, for an honest and earnest effort to arrive at verification procedures that will ensure that an agreement or agreements to make Europe free of a whole range of nuclear weapons can be trustworthy and politically acceptable. The difficulties and obstacles that will arise should not be minimized, but if there is a will, they should and will be overcome.

The other problem that stands in the way of an INF agreement is of a different character. Two assumptions are made: (1) Western Europe's security depends on the American nuclear umbrella, which will be seriously if not essentially affected by the elimination of INF, and (2) nuclear weapons are indispensable to Western Europe's security because the Warsaw Treaty countries enjoy an enormous superiority in conventional weapons.

This author is certainly not the most qualified person to address those two assertions. But I venture an opinion. The absence of INF in the European theater would diminish somewhat the options open to NATO to apply the doctrine of "flexible response." Some of the flexibility would be gone, true, but Western Europe would continue to be protected by nuclear weapons, particularly intercontinental ballistic missiles based on American soil and sea-launched missiles—not to mention the British and French nuclear forces, which will not be directly affected by any United States-USSR INF agreement (in another positive development).

The superiority of the Warsaw Treaty's conventional forces over NATO's has been mentioned time and time again, almost always by Western sources, in explaining or justifying the need to rely on nuclear weapons for the defense of Western Europe. It is raised now as an additional argument to oppose, or at least question, the advisability of totally renouncing INF in Europe. In that case, it is argued, Western Europe would be at the mercy of the East and its independence and full sovereignty would disappear, if not by an outright invasion, little by little because of irresistible pressures.

I think the time has come to deal squarely and forcefully with this issue. The need to eliminate nuclear weapons from the European theater does not obviate the need to also deal with conventional forces. Conventional weapons do kill, too, and terribly so. I hope I will not be misunderstood if I say that we, in the Third World, tend to look at conventional weapons in a different light, not because to die from a bullet wound is better than to perish in a nuclear exchange, but because the consequences of a conventional war do not affect other regions of the world, as a nuclear holocaust obviously could.

Conventional forces in Europe should not remain outside the effort to increase security in Europe. On the contrary, they should be an important element in that effort. But there should not be any linkage between conventional and nuclear forces.

Even the assumption of Warsaw Treaty superiority is open to question. The matter has been studied many times and the answers differ greatly. Some agree that one side has a great advantage over the other; others recognize superiority in some fields but not in others; others, finally, state that the forces of NATO and the Warsaw Treaty are comparable. Whatever the correct answer, if there is one, it seems fair to assess that, at present, Western Europe possesses enough conventional forces to deter a Warsaw Treaty attack, even conceding a certain superiority of the latter in several aspects. But, of course, this assessment is also open to question.

The conclusion, at least of this author, is that the conventional forces argument, whatever its merits, should not, must not, be used to oppose or to put obstacles in the way of an INF agreement. We are talking about INF in Europe, and we certainly recognize the right of European governments to take the position they consider appropriate to safeguard the security of their own countries. That right cannot be challenged. At the same time, we cannot ignore the fact that what happens in Europe, the region with by far the most nuclear weapons, has enormous repercussions on the rest of the world. Two world wars in this century originated in Europe. The most likely place to witness the beginning of the third would also be Europe, but with a difference: there would probably be no one to witness the end of that war.

A Europe free of nuclear weapons or on the road to such a fortunate situation would, of course, be of paramount importance to Europe— and also to the rest of the world. We hope that agreements to that effect will be reached in the near future. We know that the problems and difficulties are many, but they can be surmounted. There is no need to add new ones. Most of all, reliance on nuclear weapons should diminish; those regions that have them should learn to live in peace and security with fewer and fewer of them and not to panic when there is a chance to decrease their numbers.

The agenda in the field of arms control and disarmament is wide and of tremendous significance. Nothing, or very little, of importance has been done on these questions in recent years, but now Reykjavik has opened new possibilities. Let us not miss them. The possibility of a cessation of nuclear tests calls for a strong and earnest effort to reach an agreement that is long overdue. The question of the prevention of nuclear war, which could be tackled from different angles, awaits serious treatment in the Conference on Disarmament. The bilateral negotiations in Geneva should be pursued in good faith, with the political will to get things done and to advance towards goals convenient and attainable. The 1990s must be a time of successes. We cannot afford failures.

In the last instance, we always return to the same question: Do we want or do we not want a world with nuclear weapons? Almost all mankind has already given a negative answer. The leaders of both superpowers, possessors of the most powerful nuclear arsenals, have accepted as a worthy goal the complete elimination of nuclear weapons. The possession of nuclear weapons by anybody (besides, of course, those who already have them) is considered evil and a threat to international peace. The whole nonproliferation policy stems from that assessment.

On the other hand, some countries seem to consider them a good thing, a legitimate means of defense, a guarantee of peace. It does not seem to matter if they hold the rest of the world hostage, if they compel everybody to live with the permanent risk of nuclear devastation, as long as they consider their security protected.

No disarmament or arms control agreement is possible without some risks. That is a fact. Agreements without risks just do not exist. Nobody asks anybody to take unreasonable risks. But it is not reasonable to miss historic opportunities, when so much is at stake. It is not reasonable to dwell only on the risks and disregard the advantages that could follow from a nuclear agreement, not only for the region concerned, but for the whole of international society. If the obstacles prevail, one has the right to question if there really exists a true commitment to the reduction and eventual abolition of nuclear weapons.

I think the hopes and aspirations of the great majority of the world are well expressed in the message that the leaders known as "The Six" addressed to the heads of government of the United States and the Soviet Union at the end of 1986:

> However, the Reykjavik meeting demonstrated that it is possible, given political vision and commitment, to go beyond old doctrines and to break new ground in nuclear arms control and disarmament. It is heartening that the proposals from Reykjavik are still on the table and have not been withdrawn. 1987 therefore provides an opportunity for the Soviet Union and the United States to agree on a number of important disarmament measures, including deep cuts in nuclear arsenals. We urge the leaders of these two nations to take advantage of that opportunity and to build on the understanding of Reykjavik, without any weakening of the commitments made there. As long as agreement is not reached, the nuclear arms race will

ineluctably continue to escalate and the survival of all of us will become more and more precarious.[1]

A few days ago, The Six, recalling their first statement, issued three years ago, on 22 May 1984, said:

Today, we make an appeal not to jeopardize the opportunity to start a process of nuclear disarmament. . . . *Disarmament negotiations are now at a crucial point.* . . . An agreement to eliminate all intermediate nuclear forces from Europe would be of considerable significance and would constitute *the crossing of an important psychological threshold.* . . . For too long, fear and mistrust have prevented progress in disarmament. Arms and fears feed on each other. Now is the time to break this vicious circle and lay the foundation for a more secure world. *The present momentum should not be lost.*" [Italics added.][2]

Notes

1. CD/739.
2. A/42/319-S/18894.

NUCLEAR WEAPONS AND INTERNATIONAL SECURITY

*Maharajakrishna Rasgotra**

Earlier speakers . . . referred to the encounter between President Reagan and General Secretary Gorbachev at Reykjavik in October 1986 as if it had been some kind of breakthrough in nuclear-arms control. The reality is different and it is not much use putting a gloss of success over what was nothing short of a fiasco.

That the meeting was a dismal failure is borne out fully by the testimony of the participants. Secretary of State George Shultz repeatedly described Reykjavik as a "disappointment," adding on one occasion that President Reagan was right in walking away from the meeting. Donald Regan, then White House chief of staff, said at the Keflavik airport: "the Soviets finally showed their hand; it showed them up for what they are. . . . there will not be another summit in the near future as far as I can see." From the other side, General Secretary Gorbachev himself stated to the Czechoslovak paper Rude Pravo: "We have not moved an inch closer to an arms reduction agreement despite the efforts made by the USSR."

In his speech on the Soviet television on 22 October 1986, Mr. Gorbachev described the results of Reykjavik as comprising two half-truths: the first half of the truth, he said, was that nuclear disarmament was possible and that the leaders had agreed on the complete eradication of strategic weapons and the eradication of medium-range missiles in Europe. The other was that American insistence on proceeding with SDI had prevented the superpowers from reaching a meaningful agreement. Two half-truths seldom add up to a whole truth; the sum in this case is that the nuclear-arms race is about to enter outer space and the one worthwhile existing nuclear-arms control agreement, namely, the antiballistic missile (ABM) Treaty, is in jeopardy.

In a sense, outer space is already militarized; 90 percent of the more than 2,000 satellites orbiting the Earth have military uses. But the projected deployment in outer space of battle stations carrying lasers, beam weapons, and other nuclear and nonnuclear engines of war will be a very different thing qualitatively, and it may wreck the last chance of bringing

---

*Maharajakrishna Rasgotra was Foreign Secretary of India from 1981 to 1984.

the nuclear-arms race under control and ending it. I am reminded of a phrase used by Colonel General Nikolai F. Chervov of the Soviet Union to describe the situation: "Mankind," he said graphically, "will race itself into a trap."

A number of developments since Reykjavik indicate a hardening of attitudes on both sides. For example, the Soviet Union has given up its unilateral moratorium on nuclear tests. It is difficult to blame that country, for its unilateral stoppage of tests did not evoke from the United States and other nuclear weapon powers a constructive response. The ending of the Soviet moratorium is nevertheless a setback. The United States abandonment of SALT II is even more disconcerting. Although the SALT II agreement, the result of prolonged negotiations, had never been ratified, for almost a decade both the United States and the USSR had adhered to the limits it stipulated. Unilateral American abandonment of SALT II cannot but be a blow to international nuclear arms control efforts. Finally, the United States has carried out a couple of tests of SDI components, which can only be considered as violations of the ABM Treaty —and that does not bode well for the future.

SDI is no longer a mere research program in search of justification and funds; it is already underway, and efforts hastening the deployment of its early phases should not come as a surprise. In the grim picture of nuclear confrontation between the two great powers, that prospect is nothing short of a strategic calamity.

Before SDI, the two nuclear giants had managed their confrontation within the framework of shared strategic doctrines: deterrence, mutual assured destruction, stability, and so forth. They are flawed doctrines, but since they were shared by both sides, there was hope that the superpowers would work together to curb and reverse the nuclear arms race. Now, under the impulse of technology, one side has unilaterally effected a change of strategy, which is bound to cause alarm to the other and set it off on a search for countermeasures. The nuclear arms race will be stepped up, giving rise to fresh tensions and dangers.

The ABM Treaty quite clearly prohibits testing, development, or deployment of ABM systems or components that are space-based. The language of the Treaty is simple and straightforward and only one interpretation of it is possible—the straight and narrow one. That was the view, too, of the United States government until October 1985. Indeed, it was on the basis of that interpretation that the U.S. Senate had approved ratification of the Treaty, as Senator Sam Nunn, Chairman of the Senate Armed Services Committee, has asserted in Washington. In the words of

Gerard Smith, one of the gentlemen who negotiated the Treaty, "Any different or new reading of its meaning would make the ABM Treaty a dead letter." In these perilous times, do the great powers of the day wish to proceed in their dealings with one another by violating the few laboriously negotiated past agreements?

I came of age with the explosion of the first nuclear bomb, in 1945. In these last 42 years, I have witnessed many shifts of power from one country or one part of the world to another. The lesson of the history of these four decades is that the condition of advantage in nuclear prowess, if it exists at all, is an entirely transient one, and in the race of nuclear arms, nothing that one side can achieve is beyond the other's reach for long.

Lt. General Daniel Graham of the United States has told us that SDI is a change of strategy and that his country will go ahead and deploy strategic defenses. If the experiment succeeds and the Americans conclude that in the event of an attack they can defend themselves against a certain percentage of Soviet missiles, they will reduce their own offensive missiles by that percentage. The Soviet Union, the general added, can then start reducing a similar number of its strategic missiles. This sounds like a tale from the times of Rome and Carthage. In the nuclear age, I am afraid there is no way one great power can impose arms reductions on another.

In the face of the American SDI, the Soviet Union, until such time as it is in a position to deploy equivalent strategic defenses of its own, is left with but one option: to steeply increase its stockpile of offensive missiles. Highly placed Soviet authorities have said so on many occasions. Many Americans also concede that in similar circumstances this is precisely what they would do. Clearly, we cannot have both "Star Wars" and nuclear-arms control; the two simply do not go together.

In the last three or four decades, the world has missed many opportunities to reach genuine nuclear arms control agreements. In the early 1960s, for example, a real opportunity of achieving a comprehensive test ban was allowed to slip and nuclear arsenals expanded as a result. In the early 1970s, the American decision to produce and deploy MIRVS (multiple, independently targetable re-entry vehicles) introduced a qualitative change into the nuclear arms race and the stockpiles grew further in size and sophistication. We are at a similar juncture now, and SDI could lead to a doubling or tripling of stockpiles in a decade.

Between them, NATO and the Warsaw Treaty account for some 60,000 nuclear warheads. There is a concentration of some 15,000 to 20,000 of these engines of doom in the densely populated and comparatively small subcontinent of Europe. It occurs to me that the number of nuclear weapons in battle array in and around the European theater is almost as great as the number of tanks of NATO and the Warsaw Treaty in the same theater. This latter is estimated at around 23,000.

What has brought the world's leading powers to this—that they treat weapons of doom at par with the more conventional wherewithal of war? What are all these nuclear weapons for? Whom will they defend and what national interest can their use possibly serve?

Last year, a picayune nuclear mishap at Chernobyl was said to have contaminated milk supplies in far away California. Imagine the effects on Western European populations of the detonation, over Soviet territory, of 100 or more American strategic warheads. What would those detonations do to milk supplies in the United States? It might make for some nuclear sanity if our strategic planners were to have some objective studies made of the boomerang effects, on the perpetrator itself, of a sizeable nuclear first strike, no matter in which part of the world.

We must seriously examine the military role of nuclear weapons. We must examine, too, the impact of weapons that cannot be used in war on international politics and security. The truth is that this ultimate weapon has radically altered the nature of warfare. It has made war unthinkable not only militarily and morally, but also biologically.

But great and powerful nations continue to produce these weapons to accommodate new advances in technology and also, perhaps, to respond to economic and industrial pressures at home. They then use them for psychological warfare against one another and against the rest of the world. They use them, too, as bargaining chips in arms control negotiations, which results in the magnification of the arsenals and in fresh complications in the negotiations. Technology is no longer an instrument of policy; it has become a substitute for it.

No nuclear exchange could make the least contribution to Europe's defense, and it is impossible to think of an exchange between the East and the West that could not cause unimaginable loss of life and property in Europe. And yet NATO's war strategies are based on the option to initiate a nuclear exchange and, as I mentioned, it is in and around Europe that there is the largest concentration of nuclear weapons. At what level would human society survive a nuclear exchange in the area?

The medical profession has informed the world that there would be no medical aid available after a nuclear exchange. Scientific opinion is divided: some think that the phenomenon of nuclear winter, brought on by a moderate exchange, would obliterate life in large parts of the Earth: others are of the view that human life would survive even a substantial exchange. The world's economists have yet to speak: they should tell us what kind of economic depression would follow a nuclear exchange in Europe and whether the economy could recover. I suggest that the United Nations Secretary General set up, as a preparatory measure for the third special session on disarmament next year, a representative group of economic experts to prepare a report on the possible impact of a nuclear exchange on the economies of Europe, the United States, the Soviet Union, and the rest of the world.

Of the many myths and fallacies propagated by nuclear strategists, there is none more foolish in my view than the one that couples Europe's defense to the nuclear clout of the United States. It may have had some validity when the United States was the sole possessor of nuclear weapons, but once the Soviet Union acquired retaliatory nuclear capacity, Washington's guarantee of Europe's nuclear defense ceased to have any meaning or credibility. Charles de Gaulle was the only European statesman to perceive and acknowledge this reality. He said in the 1950s that no American president would initiate a nuclear exchange to protect Hamburg, Brussels, or Paris, because it would invite retaliatory attacks on Chicago, Los Angeles, or New York.

It seems to me that the very premise of plans for the nuclear defense of Europe is false, that is, it is incorrect to assume that the Soviet Union is hell-bent on conquering Western Europe and that an onslaught of Soviet armies could be resisted only by nuclear arms. It strains credibility that the Soviet Union would embark on such an adventure. What would the Soviet Union gain by undertaking a guerrilla war? Besides, developments within the Soviet Union indicate an unprecedented trend toward openness and liberalism within the country and for conciliation and cooperation with the outside world. At any rate, NATO's conventional forces have the means to knock out every single intruding Russian tank and frustrate the dreaded onslaught; and in manpower, finance, technology, and conventional arms, Western Europe commands resources at least equal to those of the Soviet Union. This is a case of a false premise leading to a false doctrine.

Europe has a major role to play in strengthening world peace and, of course, it needs defense. However, for Europe to play its role, its defense must be independent. Only then will Europe be the important factor it ought to be for peace and harmony in the world. If the Europeans feel that a nuclear component is essential for their defense to be credible, they are in a position to provide one. I should vastly prefer a nonnuclear Europe, but the matter is for the Europeans to decide, and an independent European defense system, nuclear or nonnuclear, would be acceptable to me personally.

The ongoing negotiations for the removal of medium- and short-range non-European nuclear missiles and warheads from Europe—the zero option and the "double-zero" option—are in the news these days and much has been said about them here. I believe that these two propositions, which cover some 2,000 non-European nuclear warheads in all, are grossly insufficient. Although in the moribund arms reduction process one should welcome even a modest beginning, I wish to urge a bolder approach and adoption of the "triple zero" option: the removal from the area between the Atlantic and the USSR's European frontiers of not only all non-European medium- and short-range missiles, but also all tactical and battlefield nuclear weapons, whose numbers run into the thousands.

The latter weapons constitute, perhaps, the most pernicious threat to Europe's well-being. Their placement, command, and control are widely dispersed and they are vulnerable to conventional attack. Since they appear small and harmless, in a moment of stress or irrationality someone might decide to unleash them—and we could have a nuclear desert in this rich cradle of human civilization. Europe would be infinitely better off without them.

General Secretary Gorbachev has recently proposed a nuclear-free world; he has suggested that the United States and the Soviet Union should aim at eliminating all nuclear weapons by the year 2000. That such a world is desirable is beyond dispute; whether such a world is within grasp, I am not sure. Nuclear technology is already quite widely spread, and in another 10 years, there will be in the order of three million pounds of spent fuel available, of which roughly one-third could be separated as bomb-grade material. It is, therefore, not easy to say that in the event of a major conventional war nuclear weapons would not reappear on the scene, especially if a country with nuclear capability were faced with certain defeat. Perhaps this points to the need to ultimately abjure war in international relations. But for the purposes of this discussion, the immediate needs are the step-by-step reduction of nuclear arms and comprehensive and objective international verification machinery to monitor reductions.

There are no panaceas for the nuclear mess in which we find ourselves. *Ad hoc*, impulsive actions will not do, and even our approaches to nuclear arms control are *ad hoc*. That may in some measure be responsible for the continuing multiplication of nuclear weapons. It appears to me that the world desperately needs a long-term, global plan, for the next 15 to 20 years, with clearly defined stages and objectives for the nuclear age. A plan would help focus negotiations on real issues and reconcile the negotiating positions of the two sides. I can offer no detailed plan, but the following seven points should, I think, form part of one, and I should like to place them before this group of experts for consideration:

1. All American and Soviet medium- and short-range nuclear missiles as well as all tactical and battlefield nuclear devices should be removed from Europe by agreed stages over the next five years.
2. The Soviet Union should immediately reduce, to a point satisfactory to the United States, its practice of encrypting its missiles and both countries should strictly adhere to the ABM Treaty and SALT II until the year 2005;
3. Both sides should reduce their strategic nuclear forces by 90 percent in three or four agreed stages over a period of 10 years. This would be linked to a ban on research, development, and deployment of space-based defenses. At the end of 10 years, 4,000 to 5,000 warheads would remain, shared more or less equally between the United States and the USSR.
4. The United States and the Soviet Union should stop testing their ballistic missiles, since such tests are normally conducted to ascertain the accuracy and reliability of the missiles and thus to verify their first-strike capabilities;
5. After the above measures have been initiated, negotiations should begin on the limits to be placed on modernizing and replacing British, French, and Chinese nuclear forces. Possible reductions in these forces should be negotiated after points 1 and 3 have been substantially implemented.
6. All nuclear-weapon powers must immediately agree to a comprehensive test ban. This is a vital first step, one necessary to forestall the production of destabilizing weapons now under development, e.g., third-generation warheads with enhanced radiation effects, nuclear pumped X-rays, lasers, and depressed trajectory missiles. Without a test ban, any cuts in existing nuclear forces would prove meaningless.
7. Objective and credible international verification machinery to continuously monitor reductions and test bans should be created. The United Nations General Assembly should take up the offer made by Argentina, Greece, India, Mexico, Sweden, and Tanzania in their Mexico Declaration of 7 August 1986 in this regard, and ask them to

set up international verification machinery at their expense but under the United Nations auspices.

Who will prepare the plan and how should we go about it? In the past, the United Nations special sessions on disarmament were content to deal with generalities, and at any rate a special session would entail too large a body to agree on the specifics of a well-ordered plan. The same would apply to the Disarmament Commission. The Conference on Disarmament in Geneva is a negotiating body and for various other reasons as well is not suited to the task, which must be performed by experts who are not tied to the official positions of their respective countries. A group of such experts exists in the form of the United Nations Advisory Board on Disarmament Studies. The Secretary General could ask the Board to undertake the preparation of a draft plan to be submitted to the General Assembly for consideration.

The control and regulation of armaments is only one aspect of international security, which is, to a large extent, hostage to the ups and downs of the relationship between the United States and the Soviet Union. Their political and military rivalry and hostile encounters have resulted in the arraying of countries into hostile military blocs in some parts of the world and in the all-too-frequent eruption, elsewhere, of conflicts sponsored or supported by them in a variety of ways. Therefore, the first requirement for strengthening international security is to bring about a relaxation of tension between them.

There are four great regions in the world: the Americas, Africa, Oceania or the greater Pacific region, and Eurasia, the sprawling but integrated landmass of Europe and Asia together. It would be comparatively easy to insulate the Americas, the Pacific region, and even Africa against intrusions by a rival great power. But the conflicting interests and involvements of the Soviet Union and the United States impinge on each other at too many points in the Eurasian landmass, e.g., Western Europe, Israel, and the Arab world, and it is here that their disengagement is most needed.

The Soviet Union straddles both Asia and Europe and in many ways serves as a bridge between the continents. The Soviet Union's borders, stretching from Finland in the northwestern extremity of Europe to Japan and Alaska in the east, make it a close neighbor of many countries and of virtually each main region and subregion of the Eurasian landmass.

The United States, on the other hand, though a power external to the region, has close historical and cultural links with Europe and Israel and is deeply interested in their survival, strength, and prosperity. Western Europe is a potential superpower in military as well as economic terms and can look after itself. Israel's well-being can be assured provided it gives up its conquests and genuinely seeks the friendship of Arab States.

The United States' other interests in the vast landmass, perceived or real, are peripheral. The interests it seeks so aggressively to protect in Eurasia's problem areas, such as the Gulf or South Asia or the Indian Ocean, are in no sense vital to its peace and well-being. At best they are transient in character, as demonstrated by the U.S. withdrawal from Viet Nam. What induces American involvement in most Eurasian situations is not its interest but its political (rather than ideological) rivalry with the Soviet Union. Of course, it is a fact of international life that this rivalry exists, and the United States does not wish to see what it calls the "free world" fall under Soviet domination. But the United States is much too far away from most parts of the Eurasian landmass to effectively influence situations there, and Eurasian security has, therefore, to come from within Eurasia.

Eurasia is a landmass of many countries, races, and religions, of vastly different systems of government, conflicting ideologies and interests, border disputes, ethnic conflicts, and dramatic contrasts of poverty and wealth. Placed at the world's hub, it is a tinderbox of problems, many of which are not easily soluble. Constituents of this landmass must, therefore, co-operate together to create a Eurasian *modus vivendi*, a Eurasian compact if you like, based on an inner strength and tranquillity of the spirit that transcend surrounding pulls and pressures. The process must be initiated from within the region, and its larger and more powerful entities, such as the Soviet Union and China, the European Community, Japan, and India, should begin consultations on this theme.

The intellectual basis for such an approach exists as *Panchsheel*, the five principles of peaceful coexistence that were defined jointly by India and China in 1954. Their essence is tolerance, with co-operation added if possible, or, in other words, simply living side by side in a nonviolent way, despite differences and disagreement. These principles must be broadened and their acceptance and faithful observance promoted by all countries of the Eurasian landmass.

The role I see in this process for the United States is not one of arms, military, or financial support or technical assistance. Nor is it a role of indifference or total detachment. It is the role of a benign, peaceable, and beneficent power that wants to see existing problems resolved, but knows that it can contribute comparatively little to their resolution and must, therefore, leave the task to those primarily concerned.

The role of the Soviet Union will naturally be more direct and crucial and it will also be more exacting. That great country's intentions are not in doubt, but the Soviet Union is the largest power in the landmass and it devolves upon it to cultivate and create trust and to spread it around to all of its co-partners in Eurasia—Europe, the Middle East, China, Japan, and elsewhere.

PRINCIPLES AND INITIATIVES IN UNITED STATES ARMS CONTROL POLICY

*Edward L. Rowny**

I am delighted to have this opportunity to visit the Soviet Union and to participate in this United Nations meeting of disarmament experts. I hope that the meeting will contribute to better international understanding that will lead to a reduction of tension and will encourage good arms reduction agreements.

Under President Reagan's leadership, the United States had launched a number of far-reaching arms control initiatives. These include proposals for unprecedented, deep reductions in strategic offensive nuclear arms and intermediate-range nuclear forces, as well as a complete ban on chemical weapons. I will provide details of these initiatives in the course of my remarks.

First, though, I think it is important to make clear that the United States does not regard arms control as an end in itself. Arms control should be viewed as a means that nations can use to enhance their security interests and to support their national interests. Indeed, to be truly effective and enduring, arms control agreements must be accompanied by respect for and compliance with all the principles and provisions of the United Nations Charter.

President Reagan's Broad Agenda for United States-Soviet Relations

As true peace is not the mere absence of war, President Reagan has observed, so, too, it is not founded merely on the absence or limitation of weapons. Arms control, for example, is but one of the four "pillars" on which the United States is seeking to build better relations with the Soviet Union. The other three fundamental objectives are: resolving regional conflicts, progress on bilateral issues such as "people-to-people" exchanges, and advancing human rights.

The Soviet Union's involvement in regional conflicts is a critical indi-

---

*Edward L. Rowny, former general in the United States Army, is Special Advisor to the President and Secretary of State for Arms Control Matters of the United States.

cator of whether its global aims are conducive to international peace. In Angola and Nicaragua, the Soviet Union through its Cuban proxies is pouring heavy amounts of military assistance into efforts by the Communist régimes to crush popular resistance and consolidate their power. In democratic Kampuchea, the Soviet Union is likewise heavily subsidizing Viet Nam's military occupation. But the most disturbing example is Afghanistan, where the Soviet army itself is waging a furious war against civilians and armed freedom fighters. Soviet involvement in these regional conflicts has a profoundly chilling effect on U.S. attitudes toward Soviet pronouncements of peaceful intentions.

The status of human rights and fundamental freedoms in the USSR has a profound effect on East-West relations. Soviet abuse of fundamental rights is a deep source of mistrust and suspicion. Accordingly, we are watching with great interest the recently begun phenomenon of *glasnost* or openness. Following the recent release of some political prisoners and the relaxation of some censorship of cultural expression, we can only hope that a much greater easing of repression will take place. In our judgment, though, this will require much more than cosmetic changes. Deeds rather than mere words are needed. And unless change is pursued in a deep and consistent way, those who consider the new *glasnost* as primarily a public relations campaign will have the weight of evidence with them.

I can affirm that if truly profound reforms and openings in the Soviet system were to come about, our confidence in Soviet compliance with arms control agreements would become greater. The Soviet Union can verify United States compliance with agreements very simply because of the openness of our government, our economy, and virtually every other element of our society. The Soviet system offers us no such inherent means to verify compliance or detect strategic deception.

Therefore we call on the USSR to apply real *glasnost* to its military policies and budgets. Let the people of the Soviet Union and the world see as much about Soviet military affairs as they see about United States military matters.

Basic Principles of United States Arms Control Policy

United States arms control objectives are integrated with our defense and foreign policies to enhance deterrence and stability, to reduce the risk of all war, especially nuclear war, and to support the security of our allies.

From the beginning of his administration, President Reagan followed these fundamental principles:
—We seek only those agreements that contribute to our security and that of our allies.
—We seek agreements that reduce forces, not simply limit them.
—To this end, we seek agreements on broad, deep, and equitable reductions in offensive arms;
—Within the category of offensive nuclear arms, we give priority to reducing the most destabilizing weapons, that is, fast-flying, nonrecallable ballistic missiles;
—We also seek equitable arms control agreements in the areas of nuclear testing, chemical weapons, and conventional forces;
—We insist on agreements that can be effectively verified. Arms control agreements without effective verification provisions are worse than no agreements at all.

These principles form the basis for our efforts to bring renewed integrity to arms control. A number of past agreements, it must be recognized, were flawed in concept. These and other agreements have suffered from Soviet violations.

Problems with Past Agreements

Typical of such flawed agreements was the SALT II Treaty of 1979. Rather than force real reductions, SALT II in fact sanctioned considerable increases in the number of nuclear weapons deployed on ballistic missiles and bombers. The most basic flaw of the SALT approach was that it focused on limits on launchers and placed only indirect and inadequate limits on ballistic missile warheads and throwweight—the real measures of ballistic missile capability. Thus the SALT II accord did nothing to reduce, and little even to limit, the nuclear threat. If ratified, it would have undermined the stability of the United States-Soviet strategic relationship.

Imperfect as many earlier arms control agreements were, their faults were compounded by the Soviet Union's failure to abide by key provisions. In violation of SALT II, the Soviet Union encrypted telemetry associated with ballistic missile testing in a manner that impeded verification. It deployed a prohibited second new type of ICBM, the SS-25, and exceeded the numerical limit on strategic nuclear delivery vehicles.

The Soviet Union also violated the 1972 SALT I Interim Agreement's prohibition on the use of former ICBM facilities. Specifically, the Soviet Union used former SS-7 ICBM facilities to support deployment of the SS-25 mobile ICBM.

Moreover, with its facility at Krasnoyarsk, the Soviet Union is violating the antiballistic missile (ABM) Treaty. This large, phased-array radar violates the ABM Treaty in its associated siting, orientation, and capability.

Because of our concerns about both the Soviet Union's poor record of compliance and flaws in past agreements, since May 1986 the United States has based decisions regarding its strategic force structure on the nature and magnitude of the threat posed by Soviet strategic forces. President Reagan also determined that the United States will not deploy more strategic nuclear delivery vehicles nor more strategic ballistic missile warheads than the Soviet Union. Thus, whereas ensuring an adequate strategic deterrent, the United States continues to exercise the utmost restraint.

United States Arms Control Initiatives

Let me turn now to the current status of negotiations between the United States and the Soviet Union on arms control. The United States has put forward far-reaching proposals that could substantially mitigate the threats now posed by strategic offensive nuclear arms, intermediate-range nuclear forces (INF), and chemical weapons.

We are now working to conclude an agreement for deep reductions in INF. On 23 April, negotiators resumed work in Geneva that could, if the Soviet Union is serious, result in a verifiable treaty on INF. We have indicated we would sign a treaty, as an interim step, that embodies the Reykjavik formula of reducing United States and Soviet longer range INF (LRINF) missile warheads to a global limit of 100 warheads, with none in Europe. Those remaining would be deployed in the United States and Soviet Asia.

Our ultimate goal, however, remains the complete elimination of all LRINF missile systems on a global basis. Since weapons of this type are easily moved, their complete elimination would reduce the threat to our allies and aid in achieving effective verification.

We welcome the opportunity to discuss the total elimination of United States and Soviet shorter-range INF (SRINF) systems, as suggested by General Secretary Gorbachev in Moscow. We hope the Soviet delegation will table a proposal for discussion soon. As with LRINF, the United States principles for dealing with SRINF are global applicability and equality. These principles are essential elements of our policy and the United States will not deviate from them.

Whereas we welcome any stabilizing reductions of intermediate-range missiles that enhance security, it is necessary that we make progress in other areas as well, including strategic nuclear weapons, chemical weapons, and conventional forces. In 1985, at the Geneva summit, General Secretary Gorbachev agreed to accelerate progress in areas of common ground, including 50 percent reductions in strategic offensive nuclear weapons. Further progress towards this goal was made last October at Reykjavik.

In April, in Prague, General Secretary Gorbachev said the reduction of strategic arms was of paramount importance and called it "the root problem" of arms control. Yet when he met a few days later with Secretary Shultz, he refused to drop his insistence that any reduction in offensive arms be linked to restrictions on the testing and development of strategic defenses. These constraints are not acceptable because they would cripple the United States Strategic Defense Initiative (SDI), our hope for a more stable deterrent based increasingly on defensive systems. One point I would like to make especially emphatic and clear to this audience of international experts is that the defensive systems Reagan envisions through SDI threaten no one.

We challenge the Soviet leaders, therefore, to get at the root problem, the high levels of devastating weapons targetted against one another. For our part, the United States delegation in Geneva on 8 May tabled a draft treaty on strategic arms reductions to cut strategic systems by 50 percent according to the Reykjavik formula. This draft treaty, in addition to the overall reductions, provides for specific restrictions on the most destabilizing and dangerous nuclear systems. Moreover, our draft treaty responds to Soviet concerns over the speed of reductions by extending the period for them from five to seven years. Agreement on strategic arms reductions is possible, even as soon as this year, if the Soviet Union is ready to move forward.

Besides action concerning INF systems and the root problem of strategic offensive nuclear weapons, positive movement is also needed towards redressing the conventional force imbalance and putting into effect a verifiable ban on chemical weapons. At the Conference on Disarmament in Geneva in April 1984, the United States tabled a comprehensive treaty banning the development, production, use, transfer, and stockpiling of chemical weapons. This band would be verified by various means, including prompt, mandatory on-site inspection by challenge. At the November 1985 Geneva summit, President Reagan and General Secretary Gorbachev agreed to intensify bilateral discussions on all aspects of such a chemical weapons ban. Five rounds of bilateral talks on this subject have been held since then, with a sixth scheduled . . . .

Regarding conventional forces, too, the United States and our allies are continuing to press for stabilizing arms control. In the Vienna Talks on Mutual Reduction of Forces and Armaments and Associated Measures in Central Europe, the North Atlantic Treaty Organization (NATO) has sought assiduously to meet Soviet concerns, whereas the Soviet Union has not yet responded constructively to Western initiatives. The 23 member states of NATO and the Warsaw Treaty are currently engaged in discussions to establish a new forum for addressing conventional force stability in Europe.

One encouraging development in the field of confidence-building was the recent United States-Soviet agreement on a draft joint text to establish nuclear risk reduction centers in our respective capitals. This agreement, which was a direct result of a U.S. initiative, is a practical measure that will strengthen international security by reducing the risk of conflict between the United States and the Soviet Union that might result from accident, misinterpretation, or miscalculation. Yet another positive development was the adoption by the Stockholm Conference on Confidence- and Security-building Measures and Disarmament in Europe in September 1986 of a set of confidence-building measures, based largely on NATO proposals, designed to increase openness and predictability in military activities in Europe.

Much more action needs to be taken concerning conventional forces. As we move to reduce nuclear weapons, we do not want to make the world "safe" for aggression or intimidation based on Soviet superiority in conventional forces.

If stability and peace truly are to be advanced, progress must be made on building all four pillars of United States-Soviet relations. In the area of arms control, Soviet forthcomingness is necessary in every major category. Only when the Soviet Union begins to work in earnest on the broad agenda of international peace can it be said that it is taking the necessary steps toward creating a safer world.

Chapter 3

International Security and Outer Space

SPACE AND SDI

*Nikolai F. Chervov**

Prevention of an arms race in space was one of the central issues in Reykjavik. What is our view of this issue?

Science and technology open up the possibility of the development of new types of space-based weapons, no less dangerous than nuclear ones, based on other physical principles. Such weapons are lasers, railguns, ultrahigh frequency (UHF), and very high frequency (VHF) weapons, and others, whose lethality cannot be even theoretically assessed at present. It is upon these weapons that the United States relies for the implementation of SDI.

The plans to militarize space that are being drawn up in Washington put the security of peoples at risk and precipitate a critical situation in international relations. Should efforts to prevent the implementation of those plans fail, the arms race will enter a qualitatively new stage: uncontrollable processes will arise in the field of armaments and the risk of an outbreak of nuclear war will sharply increase. Is it not high time that policymakers stop, ponder, and ward off the decisions that would push the world toward a nuclear catastrophe?

The Reagan administration attempted for four years to persuade other States, including its NATO allies, that SDI is beneficial and even necessary to mankind. Very sophisticated arguments are invented in favor of

---

*Nikolai F. Chervov is colonel general and Chief of the Department of Treaties and Legal Affairs of the Armed Forces of the USSR.

SDI. However, in all countries there is a profound awareness of the immense danger inherent in the "Star Wars" program.

Taking advantage of people's fear of nuclear weapons, Washington claims that SDI will free the world of them. The concept of a phased transition from nuclear offensive systems to nonnuclear defensive systems was especially devised for that purpose. Its authors argue that at present the deployment of strategic nuclear arms should be continued; moreover, a space-based antiballistic missile (ABM) system or, in other words, space strike weapons must be developed. Not before all that has been completed, possibly many decades later, will it be possible to reduce or eliminate nuclear weapons.

According to that theory, the elimination of nuclear arms would first require a manifold increase in the stockpiles of those arms. By that perverse logic, the path to nuclear disarmament would lie only through a buildup in offensive weapons and the militarization of space, and besides, it would take many decades. There would seem to be no other way.

What is the purpose of this exercise? It is done in order to distract the attention of the public from the need for urgent and effective measures to reduce nuclear arsenals. Washington turns the task of completely eliminating nuclear arms upside down, reinterpreting it in such a manner as to clear the way for a further buildup of nuclear weapons. Actually, that is the current practice in the United States. It is stepping up the development of six new types of first-strike strategic systems: two types of intercontinental ballistic missiles (ICBMs) and submarine-launched ballistic missiles (SLBMs), two types of heavy bombers, and long-range cruise missiles of all basing modes. It is also developing other new nuclear weapons systems and nuclear weapons for those first-strike systems: maneuverable weapons to destroy air defenses, weapons for deep penetration of the Earth to hit silos, underground command and control posts and weapons for nuclear-pumped lasers.

That is why the United States is opposed to the Soviet proposal for a comprehensive nuclear test ban and is reluctant to agree to a 50 percent reduction in nuclear arms and strict compliance with the ABM Treaty, including a ban on testing ABM components in space. In fact, its position will not result in delivering the world from nuclear weapons, but rather in a further buildup in the United States nuclear potential.

Washington has yet another idea—to place SDI outside the negotiations, to break the inherent relationship between space and reductions in strategic offensive arms. At the Geneva negotiations, the United States is seeking to get the Soviet Union to agree to the testing and deployment of space-based ABM components concurrent with a 50 percent reduction in the two sides' ballistic missile forces. What is the objective the United States is seeking to achieve?

The United States would like, with the Soviet Union's consent and for an agreed period of seven years, to develop and test everything that would be required for deploying a large-scale ABM system with space-based elements, while continuing *pro forma* to comply with the ABM Treaty. When that work is over and the feasibility of the concept of SDI has been established, the United States would start deploying a space-based ABM system and would scrap the ABM Treaty. But under Washington's plan, the two sides during that period would have to proceed to radically reduce the number of their ballistic missiles to the level of 4,800 warheads, as stipulated in the United States 50 percent option. SDI would thus have to provide a shield against a mere 4,800 warheads, which would facilitate the development of a space-based ABM defense and increase confidence in its reliability.

The strategic offense-defense relationship is a key issue, and the prospect for an agreement is dependent upon it. There was a time, back in 1972, when agreements were signed that emphasized that relationship. The Reagan administration proposed a reduction in our strategic offensive arms, for instance, by 50 percent, and in Reykjavik the president even proposed a 100 percent reduction in land- and sea-based ballistic missiles. But the United States side now denies that relationship and talks about reducing strategic offensive arms while at the same time deploying a territorial ABM defense system, including a space-based battle echelon within that system. There is no need to explain that it is impossible to radically reduce strategic offensive arms while simultaneously deploying a territorial ABM defense.

[Then] Secretary of Defense Caspar Weinberger argued in favor of an early deployment of the first echelon of a territorial ABM defense. I, for one, believe that as soon as the first battle systems capable of shooting down satellites and ballistic missile warheads are developed in space, any hope of reducing or even limiting strategic offensive arms will be dashed.

We are concerned that Washington is playing games with the ABM Treaty. For 15 years the Soviet Union and the United States, including under President Reagan, adhered to an identical interpretation of the Treaty. Now the United States side is about to renounce it and has argued in favor of a possible "broad" interpretation of the Treaty. In actual fact, this boils down to an attempt to adapt the Treaty to the SDI concept, to find loopholes for legalizing testing and deployment of SDI components in space, and to open the way for the Pentagon to place arms in outer space. Of course, the United States decision to renounce the ABM Treaty or not does not depend on the Soviet Union, but if the Treaty is broadly interpreted, it will be nullified. Naturally, the Soviet Union is not going to help the United States do away with the Treaty, and one should not expect any concessions from the Soviet Union in this respect. Suffice it to say that without the ABM Treaty there will be no agreements on strategic offensive arms.

It is clear from their technical characteristics that the space arms being developed now are offensive arms. First, they can be used to deliver surprise strikes against the other side's most critical satellites in order to blind them and catch them unaware, thereby totally disrupting or impairing their capability to respond to a nuclear attack. Second, space arms have a long range of 4,000–5,000 kilometers. But can arms with a 4,000–5,000-kilometer range qualify as defensive? They are universal weapons capable of destroying targets in outer space and from outer space on earth.

The SDI program is designed to obtain a first-strike capability and achieve military superiority over the USSR and other countries in order to blackmail them and impose on them the United States will. In other words, in purely military terms, SDI undermines the current strategic equilibrium. This military program must be stopped (except for laboratory research and testing).

What are the dangers of SDI? It will undermine the existing agreements on curbing the arms race and on strengthening security (the 1972 ABM Treaty, the 1963 Treaty Banning Nuclear Weapon Tests in the Atmosphere, in Outer Space and under Water, the 1967 Treaty on Principles Governing the Activities of States in the Exploration and Use of Outer Space, including the Moon and Other Celestial Bodies, and others).

From the military point of view, the implementation of the "Star Wars" program will definitely annihilate Soviet-American agreements in the field of maintaining strategic stability. Today that stability is known to be based on mutual deterrence, on the understanding that neither side will be the first to launch a nuclear attack, since retaliation would be inevitable, even under the most unfavorable conditions. The "space shield" conceived by the Reagan administration, together with the concurrent buildup of strategic offensive weapons, is undermining this stability and setting the following objective: to acquire for the United States a first-strike capability with impunity and deprive the USSR of the possibility to retaliate, i.e., it is designed to disarm the Soviet Union. It means that

SDI objectively recognizes and envisages the possibility of using nuclear weapons, delivering the first nuclear strike, and winning a nuclear war. This is the real danger of "Star Wars" for all of humanity.

Obviously, the Soviet Union will have to take countermeasures, although we advocate another way—the way of disarmament, which would make SDI superfluous. But we see that the United States is striving for military superiority through SDI. This is a very harmful idea. The Soviet Union will be able to find a response; it will be able to provide for its security. This response will be asymmetrical, not necessarily in outer space and not so expensive. Yet this will create an extremely dangerous situation in which there will be no trust between the Soviet Union and the United States and everyone will feel insecure.

Mikhail Gorbachev told President Reagan in Reykjavik that if the White House was so committed to SDI, the Soviet Union could agree to continued laboratory research. Last May the Soviet leaders explained to Mr. Shultz in Moscow what laboratory research consistent with the ABM Treaty meant. What is meant is research in laboratories on Earth—in research institutions, at production plants, at test sites and ranges. It might be possible to look for a compromise on the basis of this approach and discuss at an expert level what specific devices would be prohibited in outer space.

There are no arms in outer space at present—neither Soviet nor American—and there should be no arms there; outer space should be peaceful. The 15 April 1987 agreement between the Soviet Union and the United States (signed by Eduard Shevardnadze and George Shultz in Moscow) provides for peaceful co-operation in the following areas of space science: research of the solar system, space astronomy and astrophysics, Earth science, physics of Sun-Earth interaction, space biology, and medicine.

This co-operation could be carried out through the mutual exchange of scientific information and delegations, through meetings of scientists and specialists and in other forms, including the exchange of scientific equipment and establishment of mixed working groups in each of the areas involved. With a view to guaranteeing the prohibition of the militarization of outer space and the prevention of the emplacement of weapons of any kind there, the USSR proposes the establishment of an international verification system and, in particular, an international inspectorate providing for the presence of its representatives at all sites used for launching space objects.

Should outer space be peaceful or not? Today mankind is faced with this question in all its gravity. It was prompted by the Reagan administration, which initiated the development of a large-scale ABM system and space strike weapons capable of offensive operations. The appearance of weapons in outer space will signify that mankind has reached the point of no return in the arms race. For this reason, the question of whether an arms race can be prevented in outer space assumes the utmost importance. The further evolution of the military and political situation in the world will depend on the way this question is solved.

List of Projects for Co-operation in the Peaceful Use of Outer Space

1. Co-ordination of the Phobos, Vesta, and Mars-Observer projects and exchange of scientific data based on the results of these projects.
2. Utilization of the United States long-distance space communication network to track the descending Phobos and Vesta probes and subsequent exchanges of scientific data.
3. Invitation by mutual agreement of co-researchers and/or specialists of an interdisciplinary profile on the Phobos, Vesta and Mars-Observer projects.
4. Joint research to determine the most likely landing sites on Mars.
5. Exchange of scientific data on the exploration of the surface of Venus.
6. Exchange of scientific data on space dust, meteorites, and lunar soil.
7. Exchange of scientific data in the field of radio-astronomy.
8. Exchange of scientific data in the field of space Gamma- and X-ray and submillimetre astronomy.
9. Exchange of scientific data and co-ordination of programs and research related to Gamma-bursts.
10. Co-ordination of observation under the projects for studying solar terrestrial relationships and subsequent exchange of relevant scientific data.
11. Co-ordination of research to study global changes in the natural environment.
12. Co-operation under the program of bio-satellites of the Cosmos series.
13. Exchange of relevant bio-medical data on Soviet and United States manned space flights.
14. Exchange of data based on the results of studying the changes in metabolism, including the changes in calcium content, caused by

conditions of a space flight on the basis of data obtained from space flights and on-ground experiments.

15. Examination of possibilities for joint basic and applied medical and biological experiments, including exobiology, on the ground and in space vehicles of various types.

16. Preparation and publication of the second joint enlarged study entitled "Fundamentals of space biology and medicine."

A PERSPECTIVE FROM THE UNITED STATES

*James E. Dougherty**

It is impossible to disagree with the proposition that the prevention of a dangerous arms race in outer space is a matter of the highest priority. Particularly dangerous and reprehensible would be a form of frantic competition between the two principal nuclear and space powers in which either one sought or both sought such a degree of military-technological-strategic superiority as to be tempted some day to consider the circumstances favorable for a first strike. This would be highly destabilizing, especially if one side was confident of its superiority in strategic defense capabilities and the other in strategic offense capabilities.

Arms control analysts have long assumed that the bilateral strategic relationship between the United States and the Soviet Union is in a most stable equilibrium when there exists a rough parity between the two sides. Mathematically exact equality of weapons systems is not necessary; moreover, it is not possible. Each side has a varied arsenal of weapons with differing characteristics suited to its own unique geostrategic requirements. Parity involves a constant calculus of fluctuating inequalities and compensating asymmetries. In the final analysis, the effort to negotiate an equitable distribution of power for deterrent purposes between the two nations is more a matter of achieving mutual political-psychological satisfaction that parity exists than of computing the mathematical equality of physical assets.

Ever since the mid-1970s, spokesmen on each side have recurringly accused the other power of seeking military superiority, while denying that their own government has such a goal.

Whether this is mere propaganda for popular consumption at home and abroad or whether both sides sincerely believe their charges, it is impossible for me to say. Few strategic analysts, either in the Soviet Union or in the United States, really think that the current "robust" nuclear balance could easily be upset by one side before the other could react appropriately. Each side has frequently made it clear that it is determined, and

---

*James E. Dougherty is professor of politics at Saint Joseph's University in Philadelphia, Pennsylvania.

that it possesses the means, to prevent the other from ever gaining a decisive strategic advantage. Such declarations of intent definitely have a ring of credibility to them. Perhaps—and this is to be hoped—the stage is now being set for more realistic, hard-headed, and equitable bargaining than has marked arms control negotiations in the past.

Each side must be willing to grant formal recognition to the fundamental rationality of the other side's strategic decision-making processes and to admit that the technological quest for a first-strike superiority will probably prove futile, whether based primarily on strategic offensive capabilities or on a defensive-offensive mix, so long as the level of offensive weapons is high. No one can predict with confidence. But if that level should become substantially lower, as we hope it will, then it will be highly desirable to arrange a jointly managed transition to some sort of parity in the offensive-defensive mix on both sides, as both parties cooperate to move in tandem or in parallel toward a more defense-dominant régime.

Western arms control analysts have been convinced for a long time that nuclear deterrence, both direct and extended (to the members of the European alliance systems), has proved quite effective in preventing war and in making governments with nuclear capabilities more cautious than ever when it comes to taking steps that might lead to either a nuclear war or a conventional war with a potential to escalate to the nuclear level. Governments have professed to realize that any deliberate choice for strategic nuclear war (beyond a defensive first use by NATO against aggression) could serve no rationally conceivable political or military purpose, but would be absurd and immoral. We should always keep this fundamental reality in mind when we hear either side accusing the other of harboring a desire to plan a strategic first strike. With that kind of thinking, all meaningful arms control agreements will continue to lie beyond our reach. The danger of unintentional war remains, however, and both sides should work together to reduce the chances of error, uncertainty, and misinterpretation in the handling of our command and control systems. The recent conclusion of an agreement to establish military risk reduction centers reflects growing superpower concern over this problem. Now to the main topic. SDI is a research program designed to determine whether strategic defense will be, from a technical and economic standpoint, significantly more feasible as an option in the mid-1990s than it was in the late 1960s and early 1970s.

Architectures of strategic defense are now being studied by both sides, although the Soviet Union has been keenly interested in them longer than the United States. Since 1983 several different technologies have been suggested—weapons that destroy oncoming missiles with kinetic energy (including pellet-projecting satellites and electromagnetic rail guns), a variety of lasers (chemical, X-ray, free electron, and excimer, either space-based, pop-up, or ground-based) with mirrors in space to redirect their beams, and particle-beam weapons (along with ultraviolet excimer lasers) for interactive discrimination—to distinguish warheads from other objects and to disrupt the delicate electronic circuitry in the warheads' guidance or detonator systems. In our fascination with exotica, we should not forget terminal defense systems using the interceptor rockets and phased-array radars permissible under the ABM Treaty. The fact that the USSR has been modernizing its system around Moscow is one indication that it perceives the importance of strategic defenses. No decisions have yet been taken concerning technological choices by the United States. Some technologies may be considered more or less promising within specified time-frames of 10, 15, or 20 years. But the research is far from completed. It is much too early to begin choosing technologies or to estimate the cost of futuristic defense systems.

On 23 April 1987 a panel of the American Physical Society rendered its opinion that so many breakthroughs will be required in lasers and particle beams for an effective antimissile system that it will take a decade or more for responsible policymakers to determine whether the job can actually be done. That panel did not deal with nearer-term kinetic-energy systems. Some advocates of SDI would like to speed up the decision-making process for the development and testing of such systems before the Reagan administration departs from office, so that a commitment will be set in motion that will later be difficult to reverse, even by a president who does not share the Reagan vision. Naturally, many in Congress are wary of, if not hostile to, such an attempt. Administration officials regard the American Physical Society report as unduly pessimistic. When the scientific and engineering communities divide on these matters of military technology, we softer political scientists seek probable truth in the middle. In my opinion, it will not be possible to shut off completely the faucet of space technology in the next 10 or 20 years. If we act intelligently, we can control the pace and direction. What is not feasible in the 1990s may be by the year 2020.

There has been some confusing debate as to whether the purpose of SDI is ultimately to strengthen deterrence by protecting retaliatory capabilities or to replace deterrence with something totally different—i.e., by substituting an effective shield over the nation and its population. Whatever technological choices the United States makes, its purpose will be to strengthen deterrence. Reagan wants to move away from "mutual assured destruction" to "assured protection and survival" as the best way to prevent any war. This is a very new idea.

If the Soviet Union is absolutely determined to defeat SDI and the vision that underlies it, it may very well be able to do so by adopting the "McNamara solution," based upon the premise that it will always be easier and cheaper to overcome an adversary's defenses by saturating them with additional warheads. But that can be extremely difficult. The deployment of only two layers of defense—boost phase and terminal— would enormously compound the uncertainty of calculating the outcome of a first-strike plan and require a vast increase in the number of missiles and fractionation of warheads. To my way of thinking, that would be the very worst conceivable course for the Soviet Union to pursue—worst not only for the United States, but also for the Soviet Union and the entire world, for it would augur no hope whatsoever for the future. It would lead to a futile offence-defense race, the most destabilizing of all outcomes.

If I may give advice, a vastly preferable course for the Soviet Union to adopt as a rejoinder to SDI would be to explore the technological possibilities of coping with it by choosing technologies other than offensive strategic weapons. At least that would shift the competition from the buildup of capabilities of annihilating societies and their achievements toward competition for balancing defense with defense, or with offensive capabilities aimed at defensive mechanisms in space rather than at helpless populations and socioeconomic structures on the surface of the Earth.

Both American and Soviet scientists in recent years have suggested a vast array of countermeasures that might be researched, developed, tested, and deployed against space-based strategic deterrence. These include: (1) launching dummy rockets along with real missiles, (2) developing faster burning fuels in order to reduce to a minute or two the time when missiles in the boost phase would be vulnerable to attack before the warheads separate and go onto their individual trajectories, (3) rotating missiles in flight to make them less vulnerable to laser beams or coating them with deflecting substances, (4) using chaff, decoys, and balloons to confuse the defense, (5) attacking space-based defense with direct ascent missiles and/or "space mines", (6) designing offensive warheads to detonate upon contact with defensive devices, thereby producing electromagnetic pulse (EMP) disruption of unshielded circuitry and otherwise distorting electronic reception, communication, and fire directives in defensive systems, etc. It must be conceded that any object in orbit (if unprotected) is highly vulnerable to attack, and that any object capable of being launched into space has a potential to attack objects in orbit. (That is one major reason why the United States has contended that the verification problems of an antisatellite (ASAT) ban are virtually insuperable.)

Some of the countermeasures mentioned may be cheaper to produce than additional offensive warheads in missiles with self-protecting and deceptive capabilities. Some other countermeasures that can be theoretically conjured up may be both difficult and expensive when it comes to actual engineering. This would be especially true if each layer in a multi-tiered defensive system—say, seven layers, were to consist of a different type of defensive weapons technology. Reagan administration spokesmen have often said that it would make no sense for any country to deploy a strategic defense system unless it could survive possible countermeasures and could also be cost-effective at the margin. That is why the SDI funds research to neutralize countermeasures. If strategic defense will not work, the American Congress will not support it. As you know, both before and after Reykjavik, Congress, especially the House, has sought to apply severe cuts to administration requests for SDI funds.

I should say a word about the views of the NATO allies from an American perspective. Initially, their reactions to SDI were quite cool for several reasons. They had not been consulted in advance; they feared "decoupling" and a revival of "Fortress America" thinking; they deemed the new initiative poorly timed, coming at the height of their domestic debates over intermediate-range nuclear force (INF) deployment; they were worried that a program aimed at strategic defense against ICBMs would not address European concerns over medium- and shorter-range missiles; and they had misgivings that SDI would worsen the international political climate and doom the prospects for arms control by undermining the ABM Treaty. French and British strategic planners were dismayed at the thought that a new arms race for space defense would degrade the effectiveness of their own national strategic nuclear deterrent forces. Western European governments, however, as distinct from anti-nuclear groups as well as segments of the public and the media, are not terribly fearful that SDI will necessarily be destabilizing and increase the risk of war. They are willing to explore the possibility that strategic defense could enhance deterrence and that certain forms of participation in SDI research could improve Europe's hi-tech capabilities for both defensive purposes (perhaps even more against conventional than nuclear weapons) and commercial uses. Do not forget that all strategic defense technology (apart from the X-ray laser) is nonnuclear. Moreover, Western European defense élites, convinced that the Soviet Union has been vigorously pursuing antimissile defense technologies for many years, are unwilling to forfeit to the USSR a monopoly right to move ahead in such a strategically important area. The NATO defense ministers (in whose meetings France does not take part) gave more support to the SDI research program than the NATO foreign ministers of France, Denmark, Greece, and Norway. During the last 18 months, the United Kingdom, the Federal Republic of Germany, and Italy, as well as Japan (a principal non-NATO ally of the United States), have agreed to participate in various ways in the SDI program. Other allied governments (Canada, France, and Norway), whereas refraining from formal memoranda of understanding, allow their private firms to participate. Generally, the allies wish to make sure that their own security interests are taken into account in the R and D phases of space defense and that they will be able to exercise some influence over future United States decisions with regard to development, testing and deployment.

It should be noted that when the United States signed the ABM Treaty, Gerard Smith clearly linked United States adherence to the expectation that the threat of offensive strategic missiles would be reduced in SALT II—something that never happened. Since then we have argued about the construction of the Krasnoyarsk radar, the Soviet ASAT system, and Soviet research into and prototype testing of laser and particle-beam weapons at Sary Shagan. More and more of the nonaligned States are lending credence to reports of Soviet efforts. Perhaps both sides are becoming mature enough to admit that they are keenly interested in the possibilities of strategic defence.

I do not have time in this brief presentation to delve into the technical subtleties of the legal debate over the interpretations to be placed upon the ABM Treaty, except to say that neither side worked very hard to clarify what would be permitted in the future and both parties seemed willing to tolerate ambiguity rather than foreclose future ABM developments based on "other physical principles" that science and technology might make available. In my own country, the debate between advocates of the "strict interpretation" and those of the "broader interpretation" turn on the text of the ABM Treaty and Agreed Statement 'D,' the negotiating record, the record of the Senate ratification hearings and the record of actual practice. In the debate, the international law of treaties and the constitutional relationship between the President and the Congress have often become confused. We can certainly take up this matter of treaty interpretation in the discussion period.

A case can be made that President Reagan's SDI has aroused within the Soviet Union a greater willingness than heretofore to contemplate substantial cuts in existing levels of offensive strategic weapons. This becomes clear if we recall the history of the SALT II negotiations and especially the negative Soviet reaction to President Carter's proposal in March 1977 for significant reductions. If we compare that to the Soviet negotiating positions since September 1985 at Geneva and Reykjavik, we can see remarkable changes, with both sides oscillating between realistic and unrealistic proposals for nuclear weapons cuts. President Reagan's SDI has ushered in an entirely new phase in the history of arms control. Few would deny that it has introduced a novel element into the picture and led to a "sea change" in our thinking. It may seem to complicate our task now, but it might eventually provide us with the key to resolve our dilemmas. It has already slowed United States offensive programs by prompting Congress to become increasingly tough toward MX and Midgetman.

I am not certain that there will be a scientific-technological breakthrough that will make strategic, space-based defense economically affordable and militarily effective beyond enhancing the present deterrent, but even that would be valuable. Perhaps the superconductivity revolution that now excites the world of physicists will some day make strategic defense much cheaper, more workable, and more abundant than offensive weapons. It is difficult to predict. At present I am inclined to think that strategic space defense, conceived as a leakproof shield to render ballistic nuclear weapons impotent and obsolete against populations and structures, will not be technically and economically feasible to halt a full-scale strategic attack at the high levels of offensive armaments now existing, for example, 1,000–2,000 missiles carrying 10,000–20,000 or more nuclear warheads. This is always the scenario that figures in media models of "Star Wars." President Reagan may have had that scenario in mind when he launched SDI. But since then, he has frequently indicated that in his view strategic defense should be linked to drastic cuts in offensive nuclear arms. Naturally, the Soviet Union asks why it should cut strategic missiles if the United States intends to acquire strategic defense. The United States seeks a carefully managed transition through joint action from an offense-dominant to a defense-dominant régime, carried out over a long period of time to prevent destabilizing consequences, especially fears of a preemptive first strike. There is reason to think that during the last two years each of the two principal space powers has been moving toward a more realistic position with regard to exotic defense technologies—their interest in them, their cost, and what kind of agreements might be reached on the ABM Treaty to clarify permissible research, development, and testing activities while postponing deployment decisions well into the future. Soviet spokesmen have hinted that they are not inflexible on research, development, and testing. The United States at Reykjavik seemed ready to pledge no deployment for at least 10 years. That was linked to proposals for the total elimination of strategic nuclear missiles within 10 years—proposals put forth in what James Schlesinger called an atmosphere of "casual utopianism." Since then, the focus has been on a 50 percent cut within five or seven years, not on total elimination in 10 years. The United States has moved possible deployment of strategic defense forward to 1994. All of these are items yet to be negotiated.

Almost everyone seems willing to admit that our offensive arsenals are much larger than necessary for mutual deterrence. Even at 50 percent or 40 percent or 30 percent of current levels, space defense against an all-out attack might still not prove highly effective; we cannot yet be sure, but if we were ever to negotiate downward to 20 percent or lower, strategic defense at much more finite levels of deterrence capabilities would become not only more credible, but also more politically desirable and strategically essential, to provide a guarantee of security in a disarming environment. As the point is approached at which the surprise attack that had been deterred at higher offensive weapons levels might once again become "thinkable," governments and their peoples will demand defense. It was precisely that fear of reintroducing the incentive for aggression at low armaments levels that made plans for general and complete disarmament in the period 1959–1962 stillborn. If progress is to be made toward substantial nuclear disarmament in the next 20 years—and there are causes for doubt—strategic defense will come to be looked upon as a prerequisite hedge against the possibility of cheating on a disarmament agreement, of breaking out of its constraints and embarking upon a course of rearmament, or against an accidental launch or a small-scale attack by nuclear missiles or a large-scale attack by conventional missiles. Thus whether we like it or not, the growing demand of the peoples of the world for disarmament will fuel the drive for strategic defense as an imperative of national security among many nations.

SATELLITES AND SDI

James Eberle[*]

I would like to go a bit beyond all the slogans, such as "the nonmilitarization of space," "the prevention of an arms race in space," and the establishment of "mutually assured security"—which nobody had defined—rather than "mutually assured destruction." These may be fine and necessary words, but we need to understand what lies behind them; and I plan to deal briefly with SDI separately at the end.

Military satellites already exist in space. They are playing an increasing role as the "eyes and the ears" of the military. Some of these satellites have a broadly passive role and play a part in peacetime security and the prevention of war. These are the communication satellites, navigation satellites, and observation satellites that are used as part of the national technical means for the verification of arms control agreements. Other satellites have their principal role in war-fighting. These are, for instance, active and passive radar satellites, radar reconnaissance satellites, satellites for warning of sudden ICBM attack, and so on.

The communication satellites are in high orbit; most of the reconnaissance satellites are in low Earth obit. That is, to say they circle the Earth at relatively low altitudes. All satellites are vulnerable to attack and some are more vulnerable than others, particularly those in low Earth orbit. The latter are, as I said, generally the observation and reconnaissance satellites. They are vulnerable, first of all, to attack from weapons on the ground, interceptors, or perhaps high-powered lasers or other directed-energy weapons. The communication satellites in higher, and particularly geostationary, orbit (geostationary means that they stay in the same position relative to the Earth as both Earth and satellite go around), because they are much farther away, are basically not nearly so vulnerable to attack from the ground. Even if you launch things at them, it takes some time for the interceptor to get there, so there is a considerable amount of warning time.

Satellites, all of them, whether they are in low Earth orbit or in high

---

[*]Sir James Eberle, former admiral in the Royal Navy, is Director of the Royal Institute of International Affairs in London, United Kingdom.

orbit, need to have ground links. It's no good having a satellite in space talking to itself, it has to talk to the ground. Those "down links" and the ground stations that receive them are also vulnerable to attack. Attacks on satellites may be of a "*soft-kill*" nature, that is, they don't actually involve the physical destruction of the satellite, but they involve interference with the way it works: electronic jamming or perhaps laser blinding. (If you flash a very bright light in front of somebody's eyes, they can't see for a few minutes and if you make it strong enough they may never see again. You can do similar sorts of things to satellites with lasers.) These are what we call "soft-kill" weapons. But there are also "*hard-kill*" weapons. You can attack satellites by bringing an interceptor alongside them and making an explosion (a so-called space mine) or by firing guns or beams of high energy particles at those satellites. These are sometimes called "kinetic-energy weapons," or "hit-to-kill weapons". This very brief explanation describes some of the basic facts behind all these slogans.

Now what are the options for negotiated arms control to prevent possible attacks on satellites? I give very briefly three categories.

First, you could limit ground-launched antisatellite capabilities. Both the United States and the Soviet Union already have rather rudimentary antisatellite systems. These are capable of attacking satellites only in low Earth orbit. The Soviet system in particular takes a long time to set up and to make a kill. The systems do exist, but limits could be put on their use, and their further development, particularly by restraints on testing. Limits could be put on other systems. For instance, if you limit the power output of lasers that might be used to damage satellites in low Earth orbit, you can effectively control and limit the capabilities of this type of anti-satellite system. That is one sort of agreement that one could have.

The second would be of a more fundamental nature and would prohibit both the launching and deployment of an in-orbit antisatellite system. That is a system that is launched initially from the ground but remains in space, going round either in low or high earth orbit, until required for use. Such a capability is particularly important because, as I have mentioned, the satellites that are in high orbit, geostationary orbit or, some orbits that the Soviet Union uses (called "Molniya" orbits) cannot effectively be attacked from the ground. You have to have something already up in space if you are going to be able to attack them in reasonable time. So this prohibition would be on weapons in space—active weapons, like the railgun that fires pellets, or directed-energy weapons that fire high energy particles. It should be possible to differentiate between what might be genuine peacetime uses for scientific experiment and wartime uses, by putting limits on the power output allowed in space from satellites.

The third category of agreement that might be negotiated and would help with the protection of satellites, would be a "rule-of-the-road" agreement. You may think that there's a lot of space out there and that satellites are not likely to run into each other. But, in fact, space is really getting quite crowded. We could, for instance, negotiate an agreement that would help in peacetime to remove suspicion. For example, if you saw someone else's satellite approaching a vital one of yours, you might begin to wonder if your opponent wanted to destroy your satellite; and that would obviously not contribute to mutual confidence. So some sort of rule-of-the-road agreement would be useful. There are precedents for this on Earth, for instance, the very successful agreement that was negotiated between the United States and the Soviet Union some years ago, and more recently the agreement between the United Kingdom and the Soviet Union, called the Incidents at Sea Agreement. We could have a similar sort of agreement for space.

Now none of these three categories of arms control agreements for space would be very easy to negotiate. But in my view, it would be possible both to enforce and to verify them. Verification might well be a process that would call for some international agency. I don't propose to say any more about the satellite systems. I hope what I have said may be helpful to us in trying to set out what it is we are really talking about when we use all these slogans about preventing a war in space.

Let me briefly talk about SDI. First of all, I will talk about my government's attitude to SDI, which is governed by the need—and I quote—"to prevent an arms race in space" (one of the slogans!). But its policy is guided by an agreement that was signed between the British Prime Minister and the United States President at Camp David in December 1984. It was agreed that the West's aim in SDI would not be to seek to achieve superiority; that the deployment of any strategic defense would have to be a matter for negotiation; that SDI should enhance, and not undermine, deterrence; and that East-West negotiations should be aimed at achieving security with reduced levels of force on both sides. Perhaps we may be forgiven in Europe for thinking that the President doesn't always seem to remember the principles of this agreement. Let me just say that whereas most of my military colleagues believe that research into antiballistic missile (ABM) systems needs to go ahead—a view that I share—almost none of them see the likelihood that military requirements alone would justify the development and deployment of a comprehensive SDI system.

I would just like, since I have three more minutes, to make four points of my own.

First, the supporters of SDI describe SDI as being "defensive." Any prudent, sensible military man would be extremely cautious about classifying any active weapons system—one that fires things, whether bullets or electron beams—as either "offensive" or "defensive." That classification depends on how and when you use the system.

Second, the basic aim of Mr. Reagan's SDI (and all sorts of other SDIs) appears to be to defend against a "first strike." A first strike is a preemptive strategic nuclear disarming strike on your opponent. Gentlemen, such a concept does not exist. I am one of the commanders here that has had the direct responsibility of commanding nuclear forces. Let me just give you, from my experience, an illustration. If, for some reason, which I do not understand, the Soviet Union were to launch a disarming first strike against the United States and it was 100 percent successful (which is unbelievable in military terms) and it thus took out every single American land-based missile, every air force base before it could launch its aircraft, every United States ballistic missile submarine in harbor (because when they're in harbor they are vulnerable), then there would still be enough missiles at sea in the subsurface ballistic nuclear (SSBN) force, every moment of every day of every month of every year, to fire one warhead, of between 5 and 10 times the power of the Hiroshima bomb, every 30 seconds throughout more than 24 hours. That's not necessarily how they would be fired, indeed it is not how they could be fired, but that is the nuclear power that rests completely invulnerable—and I say that as a professional sailor without any doubt whatsoever—invulnerable beneath the seas to respond to any such "disarming" first strike. So the concept of a "first strike" exists only in the minds of armchair theorists.

Third, we do have a problem in the balance between defense and offense in the strategic field. We have been defending our strategic assets for a long time. We put missiles into the ground in holes. The reason we then reinforce the holes is to protect them. We put missiles in submarines. Why? Because we want to protect them. So there is no reason why we shouldn't look at whether active defense measures should also be part of that equation. This is an area that I believe requires a great deal more study.

And finally, let me just say to you, again as a military man with some sad experience in war: "Beware of military party tricks." Just because technology allows you to do something, it doesn't become a feasible operation of war; Clausewitz said that in war even the simplest things are extremely difficult. The idea that, because you can carry out an experiment or test in which a number of ballistic missile warheads are destroyed, you have satisfactorily demonstrated that you have such an operational capability *in war*—when the system *has* to work the first time to be any use at all—is in total defiance of all my military experience. Perhaps you might ask one or two others about the impact of surprise. You might ask Mr. Sakarov why Soviet Air defenses didn't stop a plane from landing in Red Square. You might ask the captain of the *Stark* why, though he had the capability to destroy those Exocet missiles that hit his ship, he didn't do so; or the captain of H.M.S. *Sheffield*, a British ship in a very similar situation. And I say this not to criticize Mr. Sakarov of the Soviet Union, the very gallant captain of the *Stark*, or my own compatriot naval officer, the captain of the *Sheffield*. I say it because the person who has actually experienced fighting a war knows very clearly that almost never does everything go right the first time.

SPACE AND SECURITY MATTERS, POST-REYKJAVIK

*Daniel O. Graham**

It is quite likely that the Reykjavik meeting would never have taken place had it not been for the question of security uses of space, in particular the expressed United States intent to use space technology to create strategic defenses. Indeed, an entire new arms control effort was put in motion by the prospect of such defenses. The change of emphasis in strategic affairs from deterrence of war through the threat of nuclear vengeance to deterrence based on nonnuclear defenses of the major powers represents the only truly hopeful avenue for the mutual reduction of nuclear arsenals worldwide.

In fact, we are already witnessing a new view of the continued usefulness of massive deployments of nuclear ballistic missiles because of the likelihood that soon they will no longer enjoy a free ride to their targets, but instead will face effective defenses. As with any of the so-called ultimate weapons of the past, the nuclear ballistic missile will lose its attractiveness to *all* States, large and small, when that class of weapon is rendered vulnerable to defenses. As long as nations decline to defend themselves against such weapons, there will be an irresistible urge for major powers to acquire more of them and for lesser powers to acquire some of them. It is imperative that the United States and the Soviet Union shift their emphasis away from the threat of awesome destruction in order to ensure deterrence. It is essential to use our best technology to render the most destabilizing of nuclear arsenals—masses of long-range nuclear ballistic missiles—impotent as instruments of coercion by any power, large or small. This is in the interest of preventing the spread of such weapons to other powers and of preventing an increase in the chance that nuclear war would be launched by accident or by the actions of fanatics.

I am not known for agreeing with the opinions of Soviet leaders on most issues, but I would like to quote some Soviet views on strategic

*Daniel O. Graham, former Director of the United States Defense Intelligence Agency and lieutenant general in the United States Army, is Director of High Frontier in Washington, D.C.

defenses with which I fundamentally agree. General Nikolai Talensky, former editor of the Soviet General Staff journal *Military Thought*, wrote that an antimissile system is designed solely "for the destruction of enemy rockets and not for hitting any objectives on the enemy's territory" and that defenses go into action only "when the act of aggression has been started."

Alexei Kosygin, former chairman of the USSR Council of Ministers, said at a press conference in London in 1967 that "defensive weapons are not the cause of an arms race" but instead "a factor preventing the death of people." Mr. Kosygin went on to attack the bourgeois reasoning of then-United States Secretary of Defense McNamara, whose opposition to strategic defenses was primarily a matter of dollars and cents. Kosygin said: "Some persons reason thus: Which is cheaper, to have offensive weapons that can destroy cities and entire States or to have defensive weapons that can prevent such destruction? Such theoreticians argue also about how much it costs to kill a person—$500,000 or $100,000. An antimissile system may cost more than an offensive one, but it is intended not for killing people, but for saving human lives."

In 1982 Marshal Ogarkov of the Soviet Union stated in a report to the Politburo: "Strategic defenses are not only desirable, they are inevitable." I agree with the view expressed by the Soviet Staff that the doctrine of "mutual assured destruction" (MAD) promoted by the United States side in force structures and in treaties such as the antiballistic missile (ABM) Treaty is "bourgeois naïvety." It is bourgeois because its main objective is to save money; it is naïve because it calls on both the United States and the USSR to forgo forever defending themselves.

Now how does this remarkable convergence of views between the stated position of Soviet spokesmen and myself relate to the question of the uses of space in the future?

If Marshal Ogarkov and I agree that strategic defenses are both desirable and inevitable, how can either of us maintain that one kind of defensive technology, that is space technology, must be excluded from consideration? Certainly I know—and I'm sure that Marshal Ogarkov also knows—that the best defenses against nuclear ballistic missile attack would be space-based. Why? Because the best defense is one that destroys an enemy's missiles early in their flight, before warheads are released or at least while they are close together and vulnerable. Such intercepts can be made only by systems using components based in space.

The United States can, and I believe the Soviet Union can, put into space nonnuclear defensive systems incapable of harming a hair on anyone's head—Russian, American, or other—but capable of preventing terrible destruction. We could both acquire defensive capabilities, which, as General Talensky said, do nothing at all unless nuclear aggression has already started.

This straightforward logic is countered not by counterlogic, but by slogans. One often hears that such defences would "militarize space." People cry: "Let's keep weapons out of space." What nonsense!

Space was militarized long, long ago, in 1945, when the Germans launched over 1,000 V-2 missiles into space with the objective of destroying London. Today the most numerous of space weapons are the thousands of long-range ballistic missiles prepared to travel unimpeded through space to wreak terrible destruction on their targets. True, until launched, these missiles sit in silos on land or at sea, but once launched, they hurl themselves into space to do their awesome work. It makes no more sense to refuse to consider these missiles as space weapons than it does to insist that a battleship is not a naval weapon as long as it remains in port or that a bomber is not an air weapon as long as it is in its hangar on the ground.

Space-borne defenses are designed to prevent the entry into space of these terribly destructive weapons and to prevent their use of space for free rides to an opponent's territory. To say that defensive weapons militarize space and intercontinental ballistic missiles (ICBMs) do not is like arguing that interceptor aircraft militarize the air, but the bombers they defend against do not. This defies all human logic.

Another more general slogan used to stop the United States from belatedly seeing to its strategic defences claims that such an action would expand the arms race. Let us look closely at this objection.

First of all, we should examine what causes arms races. There are two factors that must exist to energize an arms race. One is the inexorable advance of technology. No nation is going to allow its armed forces to continue to be equipped with bows and arrows while all other nations are acquiring machine guns. The other factor, political enmity, is controllable. There will never be an arms race between nations if no political or ideological hostility exists.

For instance, there is no arms race between the United States and Japan or the United Kingdom, even though all of us continue to upgrade the effectiveness of our forces with improved technology. Should one of us be determined to seize territory or bring down the government of the other, there would be an arms race between us. Since we have no such fundamental enmity, we have no arms race.

It is political and ideological hostility that fuels an arms race between the United States and the USSR. So long as this hostility exists, there will be constant competition, including that for strategic military advantage. But this is an area in which the USSR must remove the obstacles, not the United States. In 1920 Lenin himself threw down the ideological gauntlet that keeps the competition alive when he declared American capitalism to be "enemy number one" of the Socialist camp. And as late as the winter of 1986, the members of the Twenty-seventh Congress of the Communist Party of the Soviet Union rose as a body and recited in unison their determination to destroy the whole world of capitalism.

Only the leaders of the Soviet Union can remove this fundamental cause of the arms race. The United States has not declared a national goal of destroying the whole world of socialism. The ideological animosity is not of our making. Nor can (or should) the United States attempt to check the expansion of its technology, especially when such technology promises advantages for ourselves and our friends in security and economic progress. Further, we must insist on private enterprise—yes, capitalism—in space, not merely statist enterprises.

We Americans, if we are smart, will go into space along with our Western allies to protect and promote free political systems and free enterprise economic systems. We will do so to provide a strategic defense much more compatible with the basic moral values of our societies than the nuclear vengeance theories of mutual destruction. And we will do so to tap the unlimited sources of material and energy in space for the economic benefit of ourselves and others. The United States must pursue its space efforts in full recognition of the fact that there will almost certainly be more competition than co-operation with the Soviet Union in space.

One might wish it were otherwise, and indeed some Americans believe that the next great United States space effort should be a joint United States-Soviet manned mission to Mars. These enthusiasts disregard the currently insoluble problems of guarding the lives of men in space beyond the Van Allen belt from cosmic rays and solar flares. They seem to be motivated mostly by the hope that co-operation with the Soviet Union in such a venture would change political realities. This is what any good Marxist would call "bourgeois naïvety."

I see competition rather than co-operation in space as a promising way to change political realities for the better. If one looks closely, one can see it already working to change the world's political scene for the better.

Space programs, primarily the United States space program, have driven technology forward at an amazing pace. Since the early 1960s, the demand of our space programme for small, lightweight and efficient computers has caused a tenfold increase every four years in our ability to process data. Our SDI program has even accelerated this incredible pace.

When I was a major in the early 1960s, I was astonished at the computing power of machines that occupied a room the size of a dance hall. Today I can carry that computing power around in my pocket.

Today, in the United States, Europe, Japan, and elsewhere, millions of scientists, technicians, scholars, and businessmen have tremendous data-processing power at their fingertips. They are, so to speak, a hundred thousand times smarter than they were 20 years ago. This does not necessarily make them wiser, and the quality of their much speeded-up work is totally dependent upon their access to data—data that is accurate.

Herein lies the leverage of technology driven by space efforts to change political reality. There is an old saying about the new technology of computers—"garbage in, garbage out." That is, the computer's power is useless unless the data it processes is accurate. And this means that any political or economic system which wishes to stay abreast of the new surge in technology must give millions of people access to a broad range of accurate data. Any system based heavily on State control of information or that permits its bureaucracy to provide skewed data must reform itself or slip backward technologically and economically.

The most profound aspect of the technological revolution that arose with the space era is development in communications. But this development has had the opposite effect of an earlier revolution in communications: radio and television mass communications. Radio and television were developments that assisted the State in controlling its people. Certainly Adolf Hitler used such mass communications with astonishing success, as did Franklin Roosevelt, Winston Churchill, and Josef Stalin. But the new revolution in communications has the opposite effect. It assists the citizen in curbing the powers of the State.

This new reality must eventually have powerful effects on all highly centralized political systems—even on my government, I hope, which has been tending over the years towards massive bureaucracies. We are perhaps seeing a reaction to this reality today in the Soviet policy of *glasnost*—a policy that may account for my being able to say these things to you today.

I believe that the most important joint effort the United States and the Soviet Union could undertake would be to launch a satellite system called "*Glasnost*." (I will gladly accept the Russian name.) Why not some *glasnost* in space? Why not place in space the entire United States Library of Congress plus the Soviet Bolshaya Encyclopedia and the works of Marx and Lenin and make it all easily available to anyone on earth? Surely, here is a way to use space for peaceful purposes and to provide to all mankind the means to determine for themselves what is truth and what is justice.

And in the field of arms control, I would make one other proposal. Let both of us, the United States and the Soviet Union, agree to change our emphasis in strategic armaments from offensive nuclear missiles to defensive, nonnuclear systems. Let us agree to defend our countries and to reduce nuclear arms at the same time. I, for one, though certainly not cele brated as a pacifist, would be happy to see United States negotiators make the following proposition to their Soviet counterparts: "We are going to defend ourselves against nuclear ballistic missiles with any nonnuclear means available. As these defences reduce the threat to our retaliatory nuclear forces, we will reduce their numbers. For every 10 ballistic missiles we can confidently defend against, we will get rid of five or more of our missiles. We want the USSR to do the same." Surely this could be done without any possible reduction in either State's security and could not be rejected on military grounds, unless one party is determined to maintain a first-strike rather than a retaliatory nuclear force.

These are my propositions, I must add, not those of my government. I hope some of you will give them careful consideration. These space-related proposals contain the best hope of a universal *glasnost* and the end of the balance of nuclear terror that governs much of world politics today.

SPACE—AN ARENA FOR PROSPECTS AND PROBLEMS

*Torleiv Orhaug**

In October this year, we can celebrate the thirtieth anniversary of space research—the successful launching of the first artificial Earth satellite. During the three decades since Sputnik 1, space technology and the utilization of space platforms of various kinds have gone through many phases of evolution. We have witnessed astonishing success as well as failures; some of the latter with severe and tragic consequences. The profile of applications and utilization of space technology covers wide areas, from research to civilian and military support functions of various kinds. These applications depend extensively upon numerous platforms and probes (of widely differing variety).

The importance of space research and space technology applications is difficult to evaluate on an absolute scale. It should also be pointed out that many question the wisdom of the enormous investments being made in space and argue that it would have been better to spend this money on Earth to solve some of humanity's difficult problems. On the other hand, one should not underestimate the effects and values that space technology applications have brought about. Such effects range from the significant "push-pull" effect on technology as such (in particular, on microelectronics) to real application functions. Furthermore, one should not overlook the fact that space offers an important challenge as the "last" frontier for mankind.

Still, within a more restricted context, the various areas of application are of more importance. These applications may be structured in several ways, though it is interesting to note that the great majority of them are related to information—either by observation or by relaying information. The first group consists of a large collection of observation satellites for civilian and military use, while the second group consists of communication and navigation satellites. Application of space technology has therefore become a significant component of the "information society".

---

*Torleiv Orhaug is Director of Technology at the National Defence Research Institute of Sweden.

This paper addresses some aspects of the prospects of space technology, while emphasizing some of the problems related to the use of space. The intention is not, however, to give a detailed analysis of the various application fields or the problem areas. On the contrary, only a few of the more important points will be elaborated upon.

The paper is organized as follows. First, some of the main lines of the evolution of space technology are pointed out. Then the main fields of both civilian and military applications are summarized, with the emphasis on observation satellites. Next follows a discussion of verification problems and the possible use of observation satellites for monitoring purposes in a multinational (regional, international) régime. Finally, some of the problems related to the militarization/weaponization of space are addressed, with special emphasis on defining space-related activities.

Space Technology in Transition

The broad pattern of evolution of space technology/space applications can be summarized as follows: development of basic technology, development of infrastructure, development of and applications of satellites/probes for research purposes, and development of and applications of satellites for various civilian/military support functions. The driving forces in space development have been many, including the pursuit of political prestige as well as the need to develop new tools for various purposes (observations, communications, etc.).

Space technology has always been a costly undertaking. Nevertheless, what started as a monopoly of a very few industrialized nations has become more and more a technology accessible to many. In general, space technology services are available to and utilized by most nations throughout the world.

Many of the previous uses of space technology could be characterized as test experiments for developing basic technology and testing the feasibility of various schemes. Examples of such experiments are found in Earth observations, using remote sensing and astronomical observations from space-borne telescopes. The transition from pioneering mission to the next operational level in most cases means huge investments ("facility class" missions in NASA terminology)—investments in the order of billions of dollars for each project. This is also one of several indications that space technology has grown beyond the national scale. In the long run, international co-operation will be the only way to solve these problems.

Civilian Uses of Space Technology:

The civilian community uses space for several functions;
—Exploration of the celestial environment (astronomy).
—Exploration of the environment in the vicinity of Earth
    magnetic fields
    Earth/solar interrelationship
    ionosphere.
—Exploration of the environment on and close to Earth
    geodecy
    meteorology
    land use/vegetation/oceanography.
—Space manufacturing.

Civilian Remote-Sensing Programs

The best-known and most utilized remote sensing program is the Landsat program. Five satellites have been launched under it. Landsat 1, 2, and 3 carried sensors with pixel (picture elements) sizes from 80 m–45 m; Landsat 4 and 5 carried sensors with a pixel size of 30 m. The coarse resolution of Landsat 1, 2, and 3 can be utilized only for detection of large (geometric) features like land-forms, lakes, roads, airports, urban characteristics, and similar large-scale phenomena. The usefulness of the observational data is, however, partly due to the spectral information given by the multispectral scanner. It should be emphasized that in ordinary photo-interpretation (as in direct vision), the scene (environment) is generally interpreted by the use of geometrical features (shape and forms, texture, shadows, occlusions, etc.). The Landsat data (and other remotely sensed data carrying multispectral information), on the other hand, are generally analyzed using spectral features. This is often efficient for land/water studies, vegetation studies, environmental monitoring, coarse urban studies, etc.[1]

The recent SPOT program (système probatoire d'observation de la Terre) is interesting from several points of view. The geometrical resolution is three times better than the best Landsat sensor (pixel size of 10 m), thus revealing geometrical details far better than previously obtained by civilian satellites. Furthermore, this improvement in geometrical resolution makes it possible to investigate civilian and military activities never before viewed by civilian sensors. Also, military targets and activities of tactical interest can now be investigated.

Military Uses of Space Technology

The military applications of space technology have been developed at approximately the same time by the two superpowers, the United States and the Soviet Union. These military functions can be summarized and categorized as follows: (1) communications, (2) navigation, and (3) observations: early warning of ICBM attack, meteorology, reconnaissance, signal intelligence, ocean surveillance, nuclear explosion detection, and geodetic satellites.[2]

In many cases, the satellite assets constitute support functions for strategic war-fighting. More and more, space functions are used on tactical levels as well, for the support of tactical forces. There is no doubt that satellite systems and functions play an important role—a role spanning many different levels: national prestige, intelligence functions, support for military C³I-functions, targeting information, treaty verification, weapon navigation, alert for surprise attacks, crisis management, and control of military manoeuvres.

The military functions provided by space technology, as listed above, are all "nonaggressive" functions. Furthermore, it is generally considered that, on the whole, they are politically stabilizing, in particular with regard to the strategic scenario. It should be emphasized, however, that the majority of the space functions above also act as "force multipliers" in the sense that they enhance the capability of existing weapons (nuclear and/or conventional). It is therefore no surprise that we can now see the development of systems intended to both destroy and protect satellite systems. Consequently, we can also consider military space technology as a significant extension of the arms race.

Since the characteristics of the military satellites, their detailed use, and their incorporation into military organization and weapons systems are classified information, it is difficult to assess the degree of dependence on such systems. It is generally considered that the superpowers are highly dependent upon their systems for peacetime use (verification, targeting, and intelligence). This is probably also the case for the gray zone between war and peace (crisis-monitoring and early warning). During war-fighting, the survivability of the space systems and functions is determined not only by the attacks on the satellites themselves, but also by the attacks on the control and support functions (launching sites and ground stations), as well as by the use of more conventional countermeasures (jamming, false signals, etc.). The question of survival vulnerability and dependence upon space functions will therefore, to a great extent, be related to the particular war scenario in question.

Observations by Satellites

The kind of information that may be acquired by satellite observations may be categorized in several ways. One categorization, with respect to rapidity of temporal change ("time-scale" or "time constant") of the phenomena or activity, is the following:
—Nonchanging data (time-scale: very large/years)
    geodetic data
    topographic data.
—Slowly changing data (time-scale: day-months)
    construction
      industries
      silos
      roads
      airports
    vegetation.
—Medium speed changing data (time-scale: hours-day)
    military units (land, sea)
    weather.
—Rapidly changing data (time-scale: part of second-hours)
    communication, radar
    weather
    military units (airborne)
    missiles, airplanes
    nuclear explosions.

Sensors for Acquiring Information

In order to acquire the data necessary to obtain information concerning the activities listed above, large numbers of different sensors are used. Many of these have been developed especially for use on satellite platforms. In most cases, the information needed concerns not only the particular radiation characteristics ("signature"), but also the geographic location of the source of the radiation activity. Most sensors are therefore "image-forming," since they record both the electromagnetic radiation (or rather one or several of the properties of this radiation) and the angle of incidence (normally given in terms of geographic co-ordinates on ground-based, on sensor and on satellite parameters). The accuracy of position information depends on both the nature of the signals and the sensors used for detection. A brief categorization may be made as follows, reflecting a mixture of both signal and sensor types: (1) geographical accuracy in the order of kilometers or more: signal reception, weather, nuclear explosion detection, and missile launch, (2) geographical accuracy in the order of hundreds of meters-kilometers: radar SLAR (side-looking airborne radar) mode, weather, and oceanographic parameters, (3) geographical accuracy in the order of tens of meters: electro-optical cameras, photographic cameras, and radar SAR (synthetic aperture radar) mode, and (4) geographical accuracy in the order of meters: electro-optical cameras, photographic cameras, radar SAR-mode, and laser radar.

Characteristics of Sensors

The primary metrics for assessing the quality of sensors are as follows: (1) resolution: ability to distinguish fine details, and (2) range: ability to cover a wide range.

These metrics can be applied to three important parameters, or dimensions, for imaging sensors: (1) spectral: spectral resolution (narrowness of spectral channels) and spectral range, (2) intensity: contrast accuracy and contrast range (dynamic range), and (3) geographical: spatial (two-dimensional) resolution and area coverage.

Many of the militarily interesting targets and activities are revealed by the detection of target shape and other geometrical details. Therefore, high geometrical (spatial) resolution is needed. The spatial-resolution power of an imaging sensor is determined by the following parameters: focal length of camera, detector resolution, satellite altitude, size and quality of lenses, wavelength of radiation, and disturbing effects, including atmospheric haze, atmospheric irregularities (turbulences), and platform stability.

The actual resolution of the best cameras in military reconnaissance satellites is subject to stringent classification. It is generally believed that camera and satellite technology permit focal lengths of several meters and this should give resolution cell size, on ground, as small as a few decimeters. For resolution values as good as this, atmospheric conditions start to be important.

It should be pointed out that cameras working in the visual part of the electromagnetic spectrum are needed for detailed investigation of ground activities. Cameras using the longer wavelengths of optics, in the infra-red (IR), do not give the same ground resolution. On the other hand, such cameras are very useful for the detection of hot objects (ICBM-launches), camouflage penetration, and underground activities. Also, any sensor system is limited in its performance. The satellite sensors are limited as follows: (1) observation repeatability: satellite orbit and satellite manoeuvrability, (2) cloud and other atmospheric conditions: visual and IR (cloud penetration), (3) lighting conditions: visual (daytime), IR (daytime and night-time), and microwaves (day and night, fairly weather independent), (4) camouflage, (5) nonmovable targets, and (6) time delay of information/interpretation.

The limitation to nonmovable targets (static targets) is important; the present systems are therefore not very useful for tactical war-fighting. There are indications that the United States is developing special mosaic sensors that should make it possible to detect movable targets like aircraft and tactical missiles.

Verification Problems

As indicated earlier, the detailed characteristics and use of military space systems operated by the superpowers are not available. The same is true for the intelligence organizations making operational use of these and other intelligence data. One of the problem areas where satellite data are used is the monitoring and verification of parts of the SALT agreement.[3]

The SALT Treaties comprise the following agreements: (1) prohibition regarding construction of additional, fixed land-based ICBMs after 1 July 1972, (2) prohibition on conversion of land-based light ICBM-launchers into heavy ICBM-launcher, (3) limitation of SLBM (submarine-launched ballistic missiles), (4) limitation of the number of re-entry vehicles per launchers, and (5) prohibition on interference with national technical means of verification.

The national technical means play a most significant role in the verification process, and it is generally understood that they comprise several technical information collection processes, including satellite observations.

The objective of the Treaties is to:

—Restrict the number of strategic weapons
   main verification method: satellite observations.
—Restrict qualitative improvements on existing strategic weapons
   main verification method: nonsatellite observations.
—Restrict developments of new missile systems
   Main verification method: satellite and nonsatellite observations.

The technical means of verification appears to consist of ground-based systems, sea-based systems, airborne systems, and spaceborne systems, whereas the technical methods are the following ones:

—Radars
   line-of-sight radars
      ground-based
      sea-based
      airborne
   OTHR (over-the-horizon radars)
      ground-based.
—IR-sensors
   satellite-borne.
—Photographic sensors
   satellite-borne
   sea-based.
—Interception of communication, radar, and telemetry signals
   ground-based
   airborne
   satellite-borne
   sea-based.

These verification methods are efficient because the introduction of new missile systems (and this is true for most weapons systems as such) has to go through several phases, such as research, development, testing, production, and deployment, and it is very improbable that a system could go through several or all of these phases without detection.

The information that might be gathered by the sensor systems listed above is as follows:

—Radars: detection of existence of missile tests, determination of missile trajectory, character of re-entry vehicles, and frequency of test used to infer propagation of system through its various phases from test to deployment.

—Early warning satellites (IR): existence, location, and time of launch.

—ELINT (electronic intelligence): telemetry data indicating status of test (size, payload and fuel consumption).

—Photographic reconnaissance satellites: information about hardware.

The above summary description indicates that the national technical means used for SALT and ABM verification are multiple, redundant, and complementary.

Although satellite observations are by no means the only source of information, they doubtless play an important role in the verification process.

When we compare the various treaties (and not only the SALT Treaty, discussed above), we find that there are a number of means of verification. A summary of such methods can be made as follows: inspections/ observations, aerial observations, periodic meetings, national technical means, review conferences, consultations, notification to other parties, reference to the United Nations Security Council, inquiries, exchange of data/information, calibration tests, bilateral procedures and on-site instruments, manned/unmanned ("black boxes").

A comparison of the treaties shows further differences among them:

—Different party types.

—Multilateral/bilateral.

—Verification/no verification.

—Different kinds of limits (in energy, geographical area and time).

—Restriction on test sites.

Comparison with Seismic Verification of Nuclear Weapon Tests

It is interesting to compare the problems of using satellite observation for verification purposes to the development in the field of seismic methods for verifying nuclear tests. The first experimental data on nuclear explosions were obtained from seismic sensors in September 1957. The use of seismic data as a means of verification for nuclear underground testing was suggested in 1958. It took, however, about 5–10 years to obtain the basic understanding of the implementation of such a verification system. The seismological resemblance between data from nuclear tests and data from normal underground earthquakes constitutes a major problem in both detection and identification.

In 1958 a conference of experts met in Geneva to study the technical aspects of nuclear detection and identification. These experts initiated the still ongoing discussions about an international seismological verification system by describing a network of control posts.

In 1984 an experiment was conducted comprising an interchange of descriptions of seismic data (so called Level 1 data). This experiment was also intended to test communication systems and procedures. Also in 1984 an exchange of raw data (wave-form data or Level II data) was agreed upon. An experiment regarding such an interchange of data, with associated signal processing of the data, is planned to take place during 1988.

This brief description indicates that it takes time to build a technological framework for utilizing technical means and infrastructure for verification purposes.

Verification by an International Monitoring Agency

In view of the importance of space observation for various control functions and the creation of mutual stability and security, it is not surprising that the idea of using space observation for enhancing international stability was discussed as early as 1961. Later, following a suggestion by the President of France, a United Nations study was conducted to investigate the legal, technical and financial problems related to the use of satellite observations for monitoring military activities by an international satellite monitoring agency.[4]

Due to the great difficulties in creating an international organization for such purposes and the special problems in the European arena, it has recently been suggested that a regional organization, instead of an international one, be set up as an intermediate step.

The main criticism of the proposal contained in the United Nations study can be summarized as follows:

—Existing treaties are either being verified by currently existing means or they are difficult to verify.

—Any such organization would not only be very expensive, but also very difficult to implement, particularly in the United Nations environment.

—It is very difficult for an international organization to solve the problem of confidence.

—Strict and undisputed rules are difficult to construct with regard to interpreted data.

—Interpretation of raw data is normally carried out using complementary information of an intelligence character; such information would be difficult to acquire, handle and use in an international satellite monitoring agency.

—The process of verification is not only of a technical nature.

It is important to realize that because of the ground resolution needed for verification, satellites in geosynchronous Earth orbit (GEO) cannot be utilized due to the large distances involved. Therefore, satellites in low Earth orbit (LEO), of the order of 400 km, are (at least for camera systems available today) a prerequisite. Continuous observations can therefore not be made of a region of interest for verification. If a tiltable camera system is available (e.g., the SPOT observation camera), an area may be observed every other day (assuming no limitation due to weather conditions). Therefore a satellite verification system is best suited for observation of conditions that are slowly changing (over several days). For more rapid changes (less than a day), this system is not so well suited.

Prospects for the Future

The preceding discussion has dealt mainly with the use of space technology for various civilian and military purposes and, in particular, for conducting observations from spaceborne sensors for verification purposes. This important use of space and space technology for improving and strengthening security among nations is in addition to the well-known uses of space (as discussed earlier). The problems connected with the development of space and the use of space facilities are of several kinds. First is the traditional use of space for military support functions, as described earlier. Even though many of these functions serve as stabilizing factors, they are also elements in strategic and tactical C^3I functions and thus enhance war-fighting capacity.

Another, yet still more important problem area is the increased militarization of space which is taking place—not only for support functions, but also for weapons functions of various kinds. The present legal régime for arms control in outer space puts up some barriers to the arms race, but in certain areas, loopholes do exist. Therefore the further militarization and weaponization of space cannot be completely controlled/limited by the present régime.

The question of ballistic missile defense is of significance for the strategic relationship between the superpowers. Also, since parts of such systems can have an additional capacity for use against targets other than strategic weapons, the systems are of direct concern to other states. It is therefore important for the entire international community to control the development of weapons in space. Another important factor is the existence of operative anti-satellite (ASAT) weapons and the development of more sophisticated weapons of this kind. To facilitate efforts to find a better legal régime for outer space, it will be necessary to identify and define technologies and weapons systems in this area. With the necessary goodwill of nations, it should not be impossible to start such a process.

Notes

1. For a discussion of the use of computers for image processing/analysis, see T. Orhaug, "Computer applications in monitoring and verification technologies," paper presented at the SIPRI Workshop on Arms and Artificial Intelligence, Stockholm, 13-16 November 1986. (To be published.)

2. T. Orhaug, "An international and regional satellite monitoring agency," *Nuclear Strategy and World Security: Annuals of Pugwash 1984*, J. Rotblat and S. Hellman, eds. (London: Macmillan, 1985).

3. For details, see: L. Aspin, "The verification of the SALT II agreement," *Scientific American*, 240, No. 2 (1979), 30–97; T. Greenwood, "Reconnaissance, surveillance and arms control," *Adelphi Papers*, No. 88 (London, International Institute for Strategic Studies, 1972); B. Jasani, "A role of satellites in verification of arms control agreement." Working paper presented at the Pugwash Symposium on An International Agency for the Use of Satellite Observation Data for Security Purposes, Avignon, France, April 1980; and F. J. Moncrief, "SALT verification: How we monitor the Soviet arsenal," *Microwaves* (September 1979), pp. 41–51.

4. *The Implications of Establishing an International Satellite Monitoring Agency* (United Nations publication, Sales No. E.83.IX.3).

Part Two

United Nations Meeting of Experts on Verification

Dagomys, USSR, 11–15 April 1988

Chapter 4

Verification in Various Aspects

THE VERIFICATION OF ARMS CONTROL, DISARMAMENT AGREEMENTS, AND SECURITY

*Robert B. Barker**

There is an intimate relationship between verification of arms control agreements and security. In the United States, and I suspect in much of the world, "verification" is a word of the moment. "Verify" and "verification" are much used, but not necessarily well understood. Successive summit meetings between the leaders of the United States and the Soviet Union, with arms control a very visible agenda item, can be given most of the credit for the popularization of the subject.

Several weeks ago, in the American comic strip "Blondie," a comic strip that has appeared daily for decades in hundreds of newspapers throughout the United States, the following appeared. In the first frame of the comic strip, Dagwood Bumstead (Blondie's husband) is at the counter of a delicatessen. He asks the man behind the counter, "How's the three-bean salad?" The man behind the counter responds, "Super . . . I made it myself!" Next we see Dagwood asking if he can try a taste of the salad. He does so and, apparently satisfied, he orders a pound of three-bean salad. The man behind the counter asks, "How come you didn't take my word for it?" In the final frame of the comic strip, we see Dagwood respond, "Trust, but verify!"

---

*Robert B. Barker is Assistant to the Secretary of Defense (Atomic Energy) and head of the United States delegation to the bilateral nuclear testing talks. Opinions expressed herein are those of the author.

At the Washington summit in December of 1987, President Reagan was seen on television by millions to tell General Secretary Gorbachev, first in Russian and then in English, "Trust, but verify." It was stated first in Russian because, we are told, it is a well-known Russian phrase. I hope our Soviet colleagues here will help us to understand the nuances this phrase carries with it in the Soviet Union. For the millions of Americans who heard "Trust, but verify" for the first time, the message was simple and clear—always verify, even when there is trust—and especially if there isn't trust: verification builds trust.

For those of us who believe in the benefits of arms control agreements, who believe that such agreements can lead to a better world, verification is not simple, and verification issues are often not clear. Verification measures that sound rigorous can sometimes be useless. Whether verification is effective or not depends on the details.

I shall begin my discussion with a reminder of why we must care about competent, effective verification and with my definition of two of the most important words in the vocabulary of this subject, "compliance" and "verification," comparing and contrasting these concepts. I shall then address the question of how we can tell whether verification is "good enough" to provide security, acknowledging, as we all must, that perfect verification is unattainable. I shall conclude with a review of the types of verification that are available and the criteria that are used to determine their acceptability.

Why Verification?

Serious arms control must reduce tension, enhance stability and increase security. These benefits must accrue to the signatories of the arms control agreements, and it is even better if non-signatories can also reap these benefits. Verification is a *sine qua non* of any serious arms control agreement.

An arms control agreement is possible without verification, but it will be one of two types. The first type is one in which there is a long-term basis for trust between the parties. In this case, the agreement is a manifestation of the sense of stability and security that has already been achieved by mechanisms other than arms control, so verification is viewed as unnecessary.

A second type of unverified arms control is one in which there is no established basis for trust between adversaries, but the arms to be controlled are perceived by the parties to have no military and/or political utility. In this case, the sense of security and stability may be fleeting; one or more parties could subsequently conclude that there is utility in the arms purportedly controlled.

Serious arms control agreements between adversaries have the purpose of reducing armaments that *do* have perceived military and/or political utility. Where there is no established basis for trust, it is essential that an arms control agreement provide the mechanisms by which the parties can verify that all parties are in compliance with their obligations under the treaty. Only when the parties can be confident that all signatories are in compliance can the agreement deliver the sought-for objectives of reduced tension, enhanced stability and increased security.

Another way of defining a serious arms control agreement is to state that it is one in which, if one party violates the provisions of the agreement, that party can achieve a significant military or political advantage over the other parties. Therefore, there is no reduction of tension, enhancement of stability or increased security unless there is confidence that no party has violated its commitments.

In order to facilitate further discussion and clarify what has gone before, it is important that we define the meaning of the vocabulary that we use.

Compliance. By "compliance" we all know that we mean that a signatory has fulfilled its obligations under a treaty to which it is a party. Judgements of compliance occur *after* an agreement is in force. Each signatory will know whether or not it is in compliance. But how is any signatory to know whether other signatories are in compliance? Perfect knowledge about the behaviour of another signatory is not likely to be available. But judgements about whether another signatory is in compliance are inevitable, whether the information available is of good or poor quality. Knowledge, sometimes imperfect, will be combined with political assessments of the likely behaviour of the party whose compliance is in question. Judgements of "compliance" or "noncompliance" are subject to error, because they are fundamentally political decisions, *not* the mathematical outcome of a rigorous scientific process.

Verification. We all know that "verification" is a process that should determine truth—in the case of arms control, the truth about compliance. Verification cannot prevent violations, but it can increase the possibility of detecting violations, should they occur. Determining the truth, the absolute truth, about another party's compliance verges on the impossible —even when the arms control agreement contains the most extensive provisions for monitoring the behaviour of other parties. In the United States this has led to the use of phrases such as "adequate verification" and "effective verification." Use of either of these phrases acknowledges that less-than-perfect verification can be acceptable. But the fact that there are at least two such phrases also helps to emphasize that in accepting anything less than perfect verification, we move from an objective standard to a subjective standard—what may be "adequate" to some may not be "effective" to others. Whether "verification" is good enough is, as in the case of "compliance," a matter of political judgment. The same facts can give rise to different conclusions, depending not only upon those who make the judgment, but upon the international environment at the time when decisions are made.

Let us postulate that we seek a world in which our individual and collective security is ensured; further, that we seek to reduce military arms in a way that results in the reduction of tensions between nations and alliances, which enhances stability by reducing the possibility of resorting to the use of arms for the resolution of differences, and which increases the sense and fact of security of all nations. Acceptance of these goals simultaneously acknowledges the reality that there are today tensions and concerns about stability and security. In this environment, we must acknowledge the reality that an established basis for trust does not yet exist between the parties to potential serious arms control agreements.

The above-stated goals, and the reality that there is a lack of trust, lead to the conclusion that verification is critical to the arms control agreements that we are seeking. For example, in the bilateral Strategic Arms Reduction Talks (START) and the bilateral and multilateral chemical weapons treaty negotiations, we are pursuing agreements under which, if one party violates the potential provisions, it could achieve a significant military or political advantage over other parties. Without verification there will be not only an incentive to cheat, if a nation is so inclined, but continued suspicion on the part of all signatories that the other(s) may be cheating.

"Good Enough" Verification

The role of verification is to provide confidence that all sides are complying with their obligations under the treaty by assuring that violation cannot occur without detection. When one evaluates whether verification is "good enough," there are two different questions that must be asked: Could a militarily significant violation go undetected? Can the verification régime distinguish between real violations and permitted activities?

With respect to the first question, there are clear elements of subjectivity. What is "significant"? What standard of likelihood should be used to evaluate "could"?

Some of this subjectivity can be eliminated by rephrasing the original question in the form: "What is the most militarily significant violation that could be undertaken while avoiding detection?" In responding to this question, not only must the potential violation be described in detail, but so also must the procedure by which detection of the violation would be avoided. Sometimes this approach is described as creating "cheating scenarios." For any given scenario, two questions must be addressed: Could a cheater be confident that detection could be avoided? Is the violation identified in the scenario really the most militarily significant one that could escape detection? These questions can best be answered by experts in the appropriate technical and military areas.

With this approach, those with the responsibility for determining whether verification is "good enough" can evaluate whether the postulated undetectable violation would constitute an unacceptable risk. If the risk is acceptable for a sufficiently large number of provisions of the agreement, one should expect that on the basis of this criterion the agreement would be deemed verifiable enough.

The problem that usually arises when using the "cheating scenario" approach, especially when describing it to a prospective treaty partner for the first time, is that this approach is initially viewed as tantamount to accusing the other party of planning to cheat. Not so! The approach seeks to give all parties confidence that even if the other treaty partners chose to cheat, nothing of significance could go undetected.

The United States delegation discussed this approach of creating "cheating scenarios" with its Soviet colleagues during the early days of the Nuclear Testing Experts Meetings, which the two nations held between July 1986 and July 1987. In a Soviet paper addressing verification of the threshold test-ban Treaty of 1974 by the use of hydrodynamic yield measurement techniques, one of the authors, who had been party to those discussions, referred to the approach I have described here as requiring that verification be based on "mutual distrust" (at least that is how it was translated into English). I have come to believe that this characterization, "mutual distrust," may best capture the strength of the approach: even when one postulates total mutual distrust, there should be a requirement that a treaty is "verifiable enough." When this can be achieved, a treaty should indeed reduce tension, enhance stability, and increase security. (I am happy to say that in Geneva today, during the nuclear testing talks, the United States and Soviet delegations have accepted that use of cheating scenarios is a valid method for evaluating the effectiveness of verification techniques.)

However, there was also a second question associated with whether verification is "good enough": "Can the verification régime distinguish between real violations and permitted activities?" This is the issue of "false alarms." Even if a verification régime can detect violations with high probability, verification cannot be "good enough" if the verification régime also identifies as violations activities that are permitted. The fable of "The Boy Who Cried Wolf" tells of a town whose people stopped responding to the shepherd boy's cries for help because the shepherd, in boredom, cried for help too often when no help was needed. In our modern era of electronic alarm systems, the same problem has been known to occur: guards have failed to respond to electronic alarms because when they had responded earlier, the cause was not an intruder but an electronic malfunction.

The threshold test-ban Treaty of 1974 is an example of a treaty under which each of the two signatories, when challenged, has claimed every time that the alarm was false. The United States has, on numerous occasions, questioned Soviet compliance with the Treaty's 150-kiloton limit on the yield of nuclear explosions. The United States based its estimates of the yield of Soviet underground nuclear explosions on the analysis of seismic waves generated by the explosion. Every time the Soviet Union has denied that the yield had exceeded 150 kilotons. No agreed technical mechanism exists to resolve these charges definitively. Similarly, the Soviet Union has, on numerous occasions, questioned the United States compliance with the Treaty's yield limitation and been told that all United States tests are in compliance. The method used by the Soviet Union to estimate the yield of the United States tests is prone to false alarms.

If the limitation imposed by the Treaty had been of greater significance to the security of both countries, surely one or both parties would have abandoned the threshold test-ban Treaty long ago. Thankfully, the two nations are now embarked upon negotiations, the objective of which is to establish a truly effective verification régime for this Treaty.

A high "false alarm" rate is sufficient to deny all the benefits intended for an arms control agreement. If the verification régime consistently produces data that are indistinguishable from the data that would be produced by a violation, there can be no reduced tension, no enhancement of stability, no sense of increased security. In fact, if a party that has complied is bombarded with data consistent with a historic adversary's violation, then the situation can, in its view, be worse than if the treaty had never existed.

Therefore, along with evaluating the significance of violations that could go undetected, it is critical that one evaluate the potential for false alarms when determining whether verification is "good enough." If the evaluation of both these criteria is favourable for a sufficiently large number of treaty provisions, the treaty will be "effectively verifiable."

Verification Approaches and Their Acceptability

Having discussed the question why verification is so important and the criteria that must be used to guarantee that verification is good enough to ensure that signatories obtain the benefits that they should expect from arms control, it is appropriate to turn to a review of the verification approaches that are available and the criteria by which the acceptability of these approaches will be judged.

Historically, verification has primarily been left to the individual parties to perform as best they could. This has been codified in some treaty texts by referring to "national technical means" or by making no reference at all within the treaty text as to how verification is to be achieved. "On-site inspection" is widely spoken of today as a potential major contributor to verification. Another verification approach often cited is "confidence-building measures." We shall discuss each of these approaches in turn. As we do so, however, it will be important to keep in mind that the acceptability of any verification approach will have to be determined both by the potential monitor and by the party to be monitored.

I owe to my Soviet colleagues at the nuclear testing talks the following formulation of the set of criteria that must be met by a verification régime in order for it to be acceptable: accuracy, nonintrusiveness, and practicability. "Accuracy" captures the concern about both false alarms and the ability to detect violations; "nonintrusiveness" makes clear that a verification régime should only be capable of monitoring information that is related to treaty limitations—that is, verification is not a licence to spy; "practicability" introduces the idea that the verification régime must not pose large costs or other significant inconvenience for the party to be monitored. "Practicability" must also be considered by the monitoring party, in that the verification régime must not be so expensive that a party could not afford to implement it. These three criteria are clearly subjective, but I believe they capture the concerns that any treaty party must have about a prospective verification régime.

Returning to our review of verification approaches, let us begin by considering verification by "national technical means." Under such a verification régime, the quality of verification is directly related to the quality of a country's intelligence-gathering capability vis-à-vis another treaty party and/or the extent to which that party has an "open society"—with a free press and routine freedom of movement within the country for nonnationals. Confidence in the compliance of a signatory can be achieved through the openness of its society or through its vulnerability to intelligence-gathering techniques. In a régime that depends solely on national technical means for verification it is easier for closed societies to violate treaties than it is for open societies to violate them. In recognition of this disparity, verification by "on-site inspection," as an adjunct to national technical means, has been sought—largely without success until very recent times. In its broadest sense, on-site inspection can imply open access without any need to invoke a charge of noncompliance or even a suspicion of noncompliance. It is startling to recall that this apparently utopian verification approach is actually enshrined in two existing multilateral treaties, the Antarctic Treaty and the sea-bed Treaty. Article VII, paragraph 2, of the Antarctic Treaty states: "Each observer . . . shall have complete freedom of access at any time to any or all areas of Antarctica." This provision is routinely exercised. Article III, paragraph 1, of the sea-bed Treaty states that ". . . each State Party to the Treaty shall have the right to verify through observation the activities of other States Parties to the Treaty. . . ."

In a very limited context, "on-site inspection" can refer to inspections that can be undertaken only after national technical means have provided some basis for believing that a violation may have occurred. The patent limitations of such an approach are often further increased by suggesting that the party to be inspected must agree that data obtained by national technical means are sufficient to justify an inspection of its territory. In these circumstances, on-site inspection has no value, since it should be expected that under any cheating scenario a violator would deny an on-site inspection on the basis that the available data did not justify an inspection.

There is a middle ground for on-site inspections. It includes the concepts of designated facilities that are available for on-site inspection continuously or at random, on-demand intervals. Other concepts include provision for a multinational panel of "judges" to determine whether the data from national technical means justify the inspection of one treaty party.

The effectiveness of on-site inspection of designated facilities must be assessed by evaluating the difficulty of performing the treaty-controlled activity at facilities other than those "designated." If it is very costly or technically impossible to carry out a controlled activity in any location other than the designated facility, then one would likely conclude that on-site inspection of a designated facility—whether continuous or on random, on-demand occasions—could contribute to "good enough" verification.

On the other hand, if it is easy to duplicate the controlled activity at facilities not subject to on-site inspection, the on-site inspection at the designated facility does little from a verification perspective. The utility of on-site inspection must be examined carefully in each case; in some circumstances it will have great value; in others, it may have no value.

The concept of a panel of multinational judges which would evaluate the worthiness of an on-site inspection request has, at first glance, a great deal of appeal. In theory, this panel would be sufficiently neutral so that an objective, nonpolitical decision on whether to grant the request would be based solely on the merits of the data presented. However, the credibility of this approach can be questioned from two different perspectives.

First, is it credible that the party that has gathered the data with its national technical means will reveal the capabilities of these means to a multilateral group? It is often impossible to reveal the nature of information learned without revealing the capabilities of the source of the information.

Second, is it possible to select a panel of multinational judges that *all* treaty parties would accept as capable of making only objective, nonpolitical decisions? Maybe. I personally believe there is insufficient evidence from the past to answer this question definitively. It is certainly true that international bodies have had difficulty in the past in making the hard decisions necessary to conclude that a nation is in violation of treaty obligations. Often we have seen such decisions become the subject of superpower politics in which the significance of the data is subordinated to ideology.

Of course, to conclude that a nation is in violation of a treaty is a more politically controversial decision than to conclude that an on-site inspection is justified. So there may be reason to be optimistic that a multinational panel could operate responsibly in such a capacity.

The first such multinational panel to be created as part of a verification régime will have a heavy responsibility. The evidence of a treaty violation can be volatile—it can evaporate before an on-site inspection if the inspectors must wait too long. A violator will exercise every effort to defeat an on-site inspection by blocking it or, at the least, delaying it until no definitive evidence of a violation can be found when an on-site inspection finally occurs. Each party to a prospective treaty which incorporates use of such a multinational panel, when evaluating whether the verification régime can protect its security, will have to decide for itself if it believes such a panel can act decisively enough to do the job. The credibility of cheating scenarios in which the cheater buys or threatens sufficient panel members to block an on-site inspection will have to be examined.

Whether "confidence-building measures" are properly described as a verification approach has been questioned by some. Certainly, an extensive data exchange, a subset of confidence-building measures, has been included as part of the United States/USSR Treaty on the Elimination of Their Intermediate-Range and Shorter-Range Missiles (INF Treaty). The argument in favour of considering such data exchanges to be an additional verification approach is that they make it more difficult to cheat. Even when only part of the data exchanged is subject to direct authentication by the party to which data are given, it is argued that the larger the quantity of data provided, the harder it is to falsify some of the data, in the hope of facilitating future cheating, in a manner which might not be detected. The validity of this argument must probably be assessed on a case-by-case basis.

Some will never grant that there is any utility for verification of any item of data that is not subject to independent authentication by the party receiving the data. For them, acceptance without independent authentication is synonymous with "trust" not "verification." It is for this reason that the United States determined that the threshold test-ban Treaty, as signed in 1974, is not effectively verifiable. There is no mechanism in the Treaty for independently validating the data on the yields of historic nuclear explosions. Yet seismic yield estimates for future tests, the supposed basis for verification in the Treaty, were to have been based on these unvalidated data.

But confidence-building measures are more than data exchanges.

Their contribution over the long term to establishing a basis for trust can be important. In fact, we have come full circle. We began the discussion of verification measures by noting that an open society is less capable of cheating without being caught than is a closed society. When a closed society adopts the "confidence-building measures" of a free press and permits free movement of non-nationals within its borders, the demands on formal verification measures are substantially reduced. We should all applaud and encourage the unilateral adoption of such confidence-building measures by those who would be party to significant arms control agreements.

Summary

I have fleetingly covered the questions: Why verification? and When is verification "adequate"? as well as the broad approaches to verification, touching on the criteria that will be used to determine whether they will be acceptable. I have left the "Who" and "How" of verification to others. Working together—bilaterally and multilaterally—to improve our common understanding of these issues is in the best interest of arms control. Unverifiable arms control is bad arms control. Undetected cheating can provide real benefits to the cheater, at the expense of those who comply. Our individual and collective security can be improved only when arms control agreements take verification seriously.

THE VERIFICATION OF ARMS CONTROL, DISARMAMENT AGREEMENTS AND SECURITY

*Oleg A. Grinevsky**

The variety of participants in this forum is indicative of one of the contemporary world's new realities—the growing co-operation among diplomats, scientists and the public in their efforts to strengthen universal security and to resolve all the related issues on a generally acceptable basis. It is becoming more evident that politics today can be realistic and efficient only if supported by scholarly research and responsive to broad public sentiments. Profound scientific analysis can help us find our way through the complex labyrinth of problems which mankind is facing at the end of the twentieth century. Public opinion, for its part, provides moral guidance, adding to international relations the element of common sense that is at times so lacking in interstate relations.

Verification is obviously not a topic picked at random. Probably nowhere else are new ideas, fresh approaches and bold solutions as needed as they are in regard to disarmament verification. More than anything else it requires a giving up of old stereotypes based on cheating, secrecy and a desire to win over the partner.

If we look into the history of disarmament, we would probably find it to be almost as old as weapons themselves. Various kinds of disarmament plans—global or partial—have come down to us from ancient history. The League of Nations, as well as special conferences, committees, and subcommittees have wrestled with these problems. Each of their decisions or draft documents probably contained some rational elements, but those rational elements could not be developed and realized since there were no adequate guarantees against cheating.

What is needed is a single, integrated verification system capable of providing a basis for confidence. The new political thinking we are applying to external factors of foreign policy translates into international reality the concept of comprehensive all-round verification as the firmest guarantee of security, which ensures unity between word and deed, and

*Oleg A. Grinevsky, former head of the Soviet delegation to the Stockholm Conference on Confidence- and Security-building Measures and Disarmament in Europe, is Ambassador-at-Large in the Foreign Ministry.

consolidates the moral foundations of politics. Verification is the main pillar of a nuclear-free world, a comprehensive system of international security, and eventually of agreements on deep arms reductions. There can be no ambiguity on that score. As long as there is confidence in strict compliance with the obligations assumed, the entire structure of disarmament will be solid.

Over the past three years we in the Soviet Union have substantially revised our approaches to all of these issues, including verification. The realities of the contemporary world are such that the survival of mankind and the security of any country can be provided for by political rather than military means, foremost among which is disarmament. For that reason, the Soviet Union, more than any other country, wishes to have reliable guarantees of its security and must be confident that disarmament agreements are earnestly complied with by everyone. This is particularly so now that the world is entering a period of deep and substantial arms reductions. On this basis, we favour the most strict and efficient verification involving both national technical means and international procedures, including mandatory on-site inspections.

The accuracy, indisputability, reliability, precision, and thoroughness of the methods used to ensure that arms are being eliminated, that obligations with regard to the remaining arms and permitted military activities are being observed, and that the prohibitions are not being circumvented are, in the opinion of the Union of Soviet Socialist Republics, the main requirements of effective verification, which must become a vital element in a comprehensive system of international security. When we hear people talk about the need for double verification our reply is: We would rather make it triple.

This position derives from proposals submitted by the Soviet Union at the fifth session of the Preparatory Commission for a Universal Disarmament Conference, in March 1928. Let me recall that at that time, sixty years ago, the possibility of achieving general and complete disarmament was being discussed for the first time in the history of international relations, on the initiative of the Soviet Union. The Soviet draft convention on this subject contained an unprecedented call for the establishment of all-round verification based on "broad reciprocity, unconditional openness and involvement of the population groups that have a particular interest in early disarmament".

For us, verification poses no political difficulties. In this area we are prepared to go as far as may be necessary to provide complete assurance that an agreement is strictly complied with by everyone concerned. For instance, in negotiating the Treaty on the Elimination of Intermediate-Range and Shorter-Range Missiles, we had proposed a comprehensive verification régime setting the highest standards in terms of openness, transparency and the extent of reciprocal verification. In many respects it called for a far deeper and more intrusive verification than did the corresponding United States proposals. Perhaps that was why the United States side did not agree to everything, but in the end solutions were found that took into account a balance of mutual interests.

The INF Treaty, which represents a genuine breakthrough in the disarmament process, has no precedent either in the degree of elaboration of procedures for eliminating nuclear systems or in the specific methods of compliance verification. Suffice it to say that it provides for six different types of on-site inspection alone.

Let us try to examine what, in concrete terms, the INF Treaty and the Washington accords on strategic offensive arms—reached as a result of Mikhail Gorbachev's talks with President Reagan—have added to our ideas of verification:

1. The exchange of baseline data, to be verified by on-site inspection.
2. On-site observation of the elimination of arms, down to agreed levels.
3. On-site monitoring of the perimeter and the portals of industrial facilities.
4. Short-notice on-site inspections of three basic types of locations:
   a. Declared locations
   b. Locations where arms remain after the agreed levels have been reached
   c. Locations where such arms used to be stationed.
5. Inspections at sites which, in the opinion of either side, could have been used to secretly deploy, produce or store weapons systems subject to prohibitions or limitations.

These provisions could serve as a solid foundation on which to build in elaborating verification systems for future arms limitation and reduction agreements. What specifically could be discussed? What are the main priorities prompted by political developments in the world?

First of all, we are within reach of concluding, already in the first half of the year 1988, a treaty between the USSR and the United States on a 50 percent reduction of strategic offensive arms and an agreement on strict compliance with the antiballistic missile Treaty, signed in 1972.

To a large extent these issues have already been worked through at the

Geneva talks. A possibility of compromise exists on those issues that remain unresolved. One of the results is a broadening of our perceptions of the tasks, the role, the principles, the forms and the methods of verification. Questions which only yesterday appeared purely academic are now shifting to the practical sphere. The question of opening up for inspection the military bases located on foreign territories has turned into an urgent practical problem. It is of vital importance to provide absolute assurance of strict compliance with disarmament agreements.

Furthermore, the Soviet-United States negotiations on the prohibition of nuclear testing are approaching the final stages of work on agreements concerning additional verification measures to promote an early ratification of the Treaties of 1974 and 1976 between the USSR and the United States. This would be an important step towards a general and complete prohibition of nuclear tests. Problems related to such verification could be thoroughly reviewed in one of the working groups at this meeting.

The negotiations on the prohibition of chemical weapons are well advanced, although frankly they have slowed down recently. In our view, the convention which is being worked out must set forth reliable procedures for verification and monitoring, including mandatory inspection on challenge with no right of refusal. An early multilateral exchange of relevant data in connection with the drafting of the convention would contribute to greater openness and the creation of an atmosphere of trust.

Everybody seems to agree with this. What, then, remains in the way of concluding the convention?

The latest achievements of science and technology make it possible to develop ever more advanced technical means of verification, which enhance the prospects for concluding disarmament agreements. Yet, the same achievements, if used to speed up a qualitative arms race, can substantially complicate the tasks of verification. Experience seems to demonstrate that restraint on the part of all concerned is needed in using scientific and technological achievements for military purposes. Meanwhile, in spite of its stated desire to achieve chemical disarmament, the United States has recently adopted a decision to start the production of binary weapons. Besides its patently negative influence on the political atmosphere in which negotiations on banning chemical weapons are being conducted, the decision can create new difficulties for verification of compliance with a future convention.

Another disturbing trend emerged recently at the negotiations on chemical weapons. A number of countries began to exempt some of their chemical industry facilities from monitoring on the argument that they were private property. Naturally, we understand all the difficulties they are facing in this connection. However, much more is at stake than the mere convenience or inconvenience of a country. Trust and confidence must be complete and reciprocal, especially in an area such as that of the prohibition of chemical weapons. Without that, there can be no equal security.

In general, control over private enterprises is a real problem that must and can be resolved. Why could the authoritative experts in this forum not think about ways to put private industry fully under effective control? In our view, this can be done if we are guided by the principle formulated by Thomas Jefferson at the dawn of American statehood: "Equal rights to all, special privileges to none."

Finally, in 1988 negotiations can begin on the reduction of armed forces and conventional armaments in Europe from the Atlantic to the Urals. Many provisions of the mandate for these negotiations, including the verification provisions, have largely been agreed upon. The NATO and Warsaw Treaty countries have agreed that this would be an effective and strict régime which would include mandatory on-site inspections and the exchange of detailed data. It would be useful to exchange, in the near future, data on the NATO and Warsaw Treaty armed forces and conventional armaments in Europe.

The problem of confidence- and security-building in Europe is closely related to reductions in conventional armaments. Much has been achieved in this area. In our view, the machinery established in accordance with the Stockholm Document for verifying compliance with confidence- and security-building measures is functioning well. On-site inspections carried out under this Document provide an assurance of compliance with the obligations assumed, thereby genuinely contributing to greater confidence in Europe and laying the groundwork for new far-reaching agreements. The task now is to develop and expand the confidence-building measures adopted in Stockholm and to elaborate a new generation of confidence-building measures. In my view, this would be a very interesting topic to be analysed by experts at this Meeting.

It is also important to intensify the work at the Geneva Conference on Disarmament with a view to adopting effective measures for the general and complete prohibition of nuclear weapons tests, nuclear disarmament and the prevention of an arms race in outer space, so that bilateral and multilateral negotiations on this subject may complement each other and pursue a common goal.

The Soviet Union believes, in particular, that the Conference on Disarmament is already in a position to begin negotiating the basic elements of an international verification mechanism to ensure compliance with a treaty on the complete prohibition of nuclear test explosions, including on-site inspection and the establishment of an international system of seismic and radiation monitoring.

With a view to the early preparation of practical proposals for such a monitoring system, the Soviet Union is putting forward the idea of an international system of global monitoring of radiation by using space communication lines. We are prepared to take a positive approach to constructive initiatives by other countries. Thus, the Soviet Union supports the proposal by Sweden for the setting up of "a monitoring station of the Conference on Disarmament." It believes that such a station can be established on a cost-sharing basis to provide an opportunity for direct participation by all interested States. The Soviet Union is also prepared to use the good offices of the "Group of Six" in monitoring the non-conduct of nuclear tests.

From the standpoint of security, strict control must play a particularly important role in preventing arms from being put into outer space. Proceeding from this understanding, a few weeks ago the Soviet Union submitted to the Conference on Disarmament detailed proposals for the establishment of an international space inspectorate, which would verify that no space objects put into and stationed in outer space by the participating States constituted a weapon or were equipped with a weapon. The inspectorate would be informed of any forthcoming launch. It is further proposed that inspection teams should be permanently present at all test ranges for space launches, and that inspections should be conducted at agreed storage facilities, industrial enterprises, laboratories and testing centres.

In the event of a suspected undeclared launch, the international inspectorate would decide to conduct a mandatory extraordinary inspection at the launch site and the impact area of jettisoned parts of the booster and the spacecraft.

The "Pax Sat" concept proposed by Canada, which provides for the use of satellites to control the non-deployment of weapons in space, can be regarded as a certain "space" addition to our proposal on the establishment of an international space inspectorate.

The third special session of the United Nations General Assembly devoted to disarmament should play a decisive role in strengthening the positive trends that have emerged in disarmament and in the verification of disarmament. This is not an ordinary event in terms of the nature of the issues raised and of the possible outcome of the session. It can offer an opportunity to each member of the international community to realize its share of responsibility for the destinies of the world.

The exchange of views at the special session should be directed towards a joint search for ways and means of achieving the goals of disarmament on the basis of a balance of the interests of all groups of States Members of the United Nations.

The problem of verification, including the role of the United Nations in this area, will also be under discussion at the session. If global disarmament is a common concern, verification must apply to all. For that reason the Soviet Union is in favour of international efforts in this area, involving as many States as possible in disarmament and in verification of the limitation, reduction and elimination of arms. In this process the United Nations should play the leading role; it must become the single centre for the co-ordination of efforts for security through disarmament.

The role of the United Nations in disarmament would be enhanced, and trust and universal security would be strengthened if, under the aegis of the United Nations, broad machinery were established for international verification of compliance with agreements to reduce international tension, limit armaments and monitor the military situation in conflict areas. This machinery would use various forms and methods of verification to collect information and would transmit it without delay to the United Nations.

We note with satisfaction that similar ideas are being proposed by a number of countries, in particular by the "Group of Six." We welcome the proposal by Finland to establish at the United Nations a "base" of military, scientific and technological data and materials provided by the Member States on a voluntary basis. The implementation of this valuable initiative would contribute to a search for mutually acceptable solutions to issues of verification of compliance with agreements on the limitation and reduction of arms, as well as confidence-building measures. It would be instrumental in strengthening the central role of the United Nations in the area of disarmament.

With a view to supporting international efforts in disarmament, including verification, it would appear appropriate to think about new and promising ways to bring about a more active involvement of the international scientific potential in the process. During his visit to Washington, Mikhail S. Gorbachev suggested to Ronald Reagan that a bilateral commission of scientists should be established which would present its views and recommendations to the United States administration and the Soviet leadership.

We would not object to similar steps being taken on a multilateral basis, particularly within the framework of the Geneva Conference on Disarmament. It would be possible, for instance, to establish an advisory council of prominent scientists and public personalities to seek solutions to the problems of disarmament on the agenda of the Conference, and to identify long-term factors of particular importance to the strengthening of international security.

Recalling the ancient maxim that harmony results from diversity, we call for a thorough international dialogue on the establishment of an international verification machinery under the aegis of the United Nations and on other topical aspects of verification; a substantive discussion of all existing ideas; and a joint search for generally acceptable ways to implement them. Our meeting should also add to the list of valuable proposals on verification. We hope that it will play an important role in developing a fruitful multilateral discussion of these subjects and will contribute to greater joint efforts on the part of all States to make the disarmament process continuous and irreversible.

PRINCIPLES OF VERIFICATION: THE MULTILATERAL CONTEXT

*F. Ronald Cleminson**

No single issue in the decade of the 1990s is likely to be of greater significance in international disarmament and arms control negotiations than verification. International meetings such as the Dagomys Conference, activities in the United Nations Disarmament Commission (UNDC) and in the Conference on Disarmament (CD), and the forthcoming special session of the General Assembly devoted to disarmament reinforce this fact. Because of this, the Canadian government has devoted considerable resources to examining the subject of multilateral arms control verification. Simply stated: agreement on adequate and effective verification is an essential, though not the only, condition for the conclusion of any meaningful arms control and disarmament agreement.

While the detailed aspects of any verification provisions are likely to be treaty-specific, it is nevertheless possible to identify a number of common elements in the verification process and to study them in a generic way. Verification can be analysed and discussed as a general process. Such examination can be particularly beneficial in the consideration of basic principles relating to multilateral arms control and verification.

The United Nations has an important and valuable role to play in examining the principles of multilateral verification. There has often been a tendency for some countries, particularly those whose primary concern focuses on negotiations relating to Europe, to assume a rather narrow view of verification. It is essential to recognize the usefulness of a broader examination of the question in order to create a universally acceptable series of principles and to benefit from the collective wisdom of a broadly based forum such as the United Nations. We should recognize those features of the United Nations that might facilitate the verification process. They include the open-ended nature of United Nations membership and the freedom of thought which is provided by a non-negotiating type of mandate for its deliberations. Because of this universal membership and its emphasis on the building of consensus, the United Nations can pro-

---

*F. Ronald Cleminson is Head of the Verification Research Unit in the Arms Control and Disarmament Division of the Department of External Affairs, Canada.

vide unique services and help to foster authoritative guidelines for arms control negotiations.

Why Discuss Principles?

The question may be asked, why it is necessary or useful to consider principles of multilateral verification. To begin with, it is a subject of growing importance: recent events lead to optimism that increasing progress will be made towards the conclusion of significant multilateral arms control agreements. The signing of the Stockholm Document in September 1986, with its provisions relating to the conduct of challenge on-site inspections, is a noteworthy event in this regard. In a bilateral context, the verification provisions of the Treaty on the Elimination of Intermediate- and Shorter-Range Missiles signed in December 1987 constitutes a major precedent for future agreements, including multilateral ones.

Discussions on general principles of multilateral verification can also help order the mind on this critical subject. They can elucidate genuine differences of viewpoint and bridge gaps in understanding. The process of engaging in such discussions can in itself also help build confidence among countries. Arms control, including verification, is a collective and increasingly co-operative activity, and one which must be fostered through a commitment to diligent research and frank discussion.

The achievement of a shared and authoritative statement of multilateral verification principles could greatly assist negotiators in their attempts to conclude meaningful arms control agreements and thereby reduce tensions and help ensure the security of all countries. This is not to say that agreeing on verification is the only concern in developing such treaties, but rather that it is an essential ingredient, and one without which there can be little hope for progress.

Sources for Principles

From what existing sources can we derive principles applicable to multilateral arms control verification? To begin with, the United Nations itself is a rich source of ideas on this subject. The most authoritative statement by the United Nations on verification, so far, is perhaps found in the Final Document of the first special session devoted to disarmament, the relevant paragraphs of which are as follows:

"Declaration" [paragraph 31]: Disarmament and arms limitation agreements should provide for adequate measures of verification satisfactory to all parties concerned in order to create the necessary confidence and ensure that they are being observed by all parties.

The form and modalities of the verification to be provided for in any specific agreement depend upon and should be determined by the purposes, scope and nature of the agreement. Agreements should provide for the participation of parties directly or through the United Nations system in the verification process. Where appropriate, a combination of several methods of verification as well as other compliance procedures should be employed.

"Programme of Action" [paragraphs 91 and 92]: In order to facilitate the conclusion and effective implementation of disarmament agreements and to create confidence, States should accept appropriate provisions for verification in such agreements.

In the context of international disarmament negotiations, the problem of verification should be further examined and adequate methods and procedures in this field be considered. Every effort should be made to develop appropriate methods and procedures which are non-discriminatory and which do not unduly interfere with the internal affairs of other States or jeopardize their economic and social development.

The importance of "verification in all its aspects" has also been highlighted within the United Nations context in successive General Assembly resolutions, beginning with resolution 40/152(O) of 1985. In these resolutions, in addition to reiterating some basic verification principles taken from the Final Document of the first special session, the General Assembly requested the written views of Member States on the subject. In resolution 41/86(Q) the General Assembly also referred the subject of verification in all its aspects to the consideration of the Disarmament Commission. At the conclusion of its 1987 session, the Disarmament Commission agreed on a preliminary list of 10 principles relating to verification. These were as follows:

1. Adequate and effective verification is an essential element of all arms limitation and disarmament agreements.
2. Verification is not an aim in itself, but an essential element in the process of achieving arms limitation and disarmament agreements.
3. Verification should promote the implementation of arms limitation and disarmament measures, build confidence among states and ensure that agreements are being observed by all parties.
4. Adequate and effective verification requires employment of differ-

ent techniques, such as national technical means, international technical means and international procedures, including on-site inspections.

5. Verification in the arms limitation and disarmament process will benefit from greater openness.
6. Arms limitation and disarmament agreements should include explicit provisions whereby each party undertakes not to interfere with the agreed methods, procedures and techniques of verification, when these are operating in a manner consistent with the provisions of the agreement and generally recognized principles of international law.
7. Arms limitation and disarmament agreements should include explicit provisions whereby each party undertakes not to use deliberate concealment measures that impede verification of compliance with the agreement.
8. To assess the continuing adequacy and effectiveness of the verification system, an arms limitation and disarmament agreement should provide for procedures and mechanisms for review and evaluation. Where possible, time-frames for such reviews should be agreed in order to facilitate this assessment.
9. Verification arrangements should be addressed at the outset and at every stage of negotiations on specific arms limitation and disarmament agreements.
10. All States have equal rights to participate in the process of international verification of agreements to which they are parties."

It is to be hoped that the United Nations Disarmament Commission will be able to bring its consideration of the subject to a successful conclusion in 1988.

The deliberations of the United Nations General Assembly and of the Disarmament Commission provide one source of verification principles. Existing arms control and disarmament treaties are another.

Several multilateral agreements have, for example, underlined the importance of co-operation and consultation among States parties to resolve ambiguities about compliance and of allowing for a role of the United Nations in this context. The Treaty on the Non-Proliferation of Nuclear Weapons, the Treaty of Tlatelolco, and the South Pacific Nuclear Free Zone Treaty have all relied upon the safeguards system of the International Atomic Energy Agency for the purpose of verifying compliance with their obligations. Generally, however, existing multilateral agreements have not addressed the subject of verification satisfactorily. This weakness has been evidenced by a number of recent disputes regarding alleged violations.

Bilateral agreements between the United States of America and the Union of Soviet Socialist Republics can also provide a valuable source of verification principles for a multilateral context. The important precedent of the recent INF Treaty has already been mentioned. In addition, two of the principles agreed on by the United Nations Disarmament Commission in its 1987 report—those dealing with noninterference with verification means and nonconcealment—are taken directly from the verification provisions of a number of bilateral agreements between the superpowers. Moreover, the attention given to verification in arms control agreements between the superpowers, as well as recent disputes about compliance, have served to emphasize how weaknesses in the verification system can undermine trust.

Another potential source of verification principles, one which has probably not yet received the attention it warrants, is research into the verification process. Much remains to be done in this area. The United Nations and its associated bodies such as the United Nations Institute for Disarmament Research have an important role to play in this regard. Moreover, we have now reached a stage in the consideration of this subject at which a serious study by a United Nations Group of Experts could lead to a significant step forward.

Some Principles

The foregoing paragraphs dealt with some of the reasons why a discussion of multilateral verification principles is important, as well as some of the possible sources for such principles. The nature of some of these provisions is suggested in the following listing, which is not intended to be comprehensive.

1. Explicit provisions respecting verification. Verification should be an integral part of an arms control agreement. The specifics of the verification system, including the implementing provisions, should be spelt out and should constitute part of the agreement. As verification often involves co-operation between the parties, clear drafting will facilitate this process. In the case of multilateral agreements, where verification activities involve co-operation between many countries, it is particularly important to be explicit about means, procedures, rights and duties respecting verification, in order to avoid later disputes.

Procedures for resolving ambiguities about compliance, which form a critical ancillary aspect of the verification process, should also be expressly laid down in an arms control treaty. In addition, an agreement should provide for procedures for reviewing, evaluating and updating the verification mechanism in order to ensure its continued effective operation.

2. Noninterference with verification mechanisms. An arms control agreement should include an explicit provision whereby each party undertakes not to interfere with the agreed methods, procedures and techniques of verification when these are operating in a manner consistent with generally recognized principles of international law and with the other provisions of the agreement.

An arms control agreement should also include an explicit provision whereby each party undertakes not to use deliberate concealment measures which impede verification of compliance with the agreement.

3. Adequacy and effectiveness. This is an extremely difficult concept with which to deal. Verification is unlikely to provide 100 percent certainty of detecting and proving every violation. The appropriate standard of adequacy for a verification mechanism could be, for example, to detect, beyond a reasonable doubt, a violation of an agreement which would permit a State to acquire a military capability threatening to the national security of any party to the agreement. This means timely detection. The verification mechanism must be capable in such a case of detecting a violation early enough so that innocent parties would be able to respond appropriately to negate any advantage that a violator might gain. It also means that verification methods agreed to, must be provided sufficient access to a State party so that the necessary data to meet this tough standard of proof can be obtained.

The ability of a verification mechanism to detect violations adequately will help deter violations. Fundamentally, countries adhere to arms control undertakings so long as it remains in their interests to do so. By detecting violations early enough to prevent the party concerned from gaining a significant military advantage, an adequate verification mechanism will help ensure that parties continue to perceive compliance with the treaty to be in their interests.

An adequate verification mechanism will also help build confidence among parties, an important factor in enhancing stability and security.

There is a relationship between the military significance of an agreement and the need for verification. In general, the greater the significance, the greater are the demands on the verification provisions. Also, the shorter the time span between the supposed breach of an agreement and the security-related effects of that breach, the greater is the need for effective verification.

As levels of forces or military activities are reduced, the importance of verification increases and the verification measures and procedures that are deemed adequate will correspondingly become more strict. As lower levels of forces or activities are reached, the risk posed by a minor, and hence less easily detected, violation to the security of other parties, becomes graver.

The exchange of adequately verified information concerning existing levels of armaments and military activities, before any reductions in levels or other limitations occur, will greatly assist in the negotiation and the implementation of any agreement on reductions. Such information, when it is verified as accurate, increases predictability and builds confidence that security will not be placed at risk by the noncompliance of other parties with the agreement.

Adequate verification of *actual* reductions of armaments or military activities, in a timely and thorough manner as the reductions proceed, is essential. Reliable verification and control at all stages of the implementation of agreements are essential.

After reductions have been completed and the agreed thresholds reached, the levels of relevant forces must be regularly and adequately verified to ensure that levels remain at or below the agreed thresholds and that forces are not restructured or deployed in a manner inconsistent with the agreement.

The adequacy of any verification system will also depend upon the effectiveness of the technologies and procedures employed for verification purposes, that is, their ability to perform the verification tasks assigned them. The scientific and technical limitations of these techniques must, therefore, be carefully examined when negotiating and designing the verification provisions of any agreement.

The technical effectiveness of a verification system also involves ensuring that any organization created to implement the system has the technical competence and capability to do so. This implies not only the availability of appropriate resources in terms of skilled personnel, training, appropriate machinery and devices, and the like, but also the acquisition and development of expertise in the area of analysis and data interpretation. Such a capability cannot be developed overnight.

The practical requirements of manpower and cost must be considered when designing adequate verification mechanisms. The significance of the human factor in the development of verification provisions is often not fully appreciated. Schemes for verification must be assessed in critical cost-benefit terms. Systems which duplicate existing national capabilities may not be essential. The use of random sampling techniques can also serve to reduce costs.

The arms control agreement in question must be sufficiently significant, in terms of enhancing security and stability, to warrant the level of technology and expenditure of resources required to establish advanced systems such as satellites specifically for verification.

The technology requirements of verification should be met by the collectivity of the participants and should not depend upon or call for the use of the technology possessed exclusively by any particular parties, notably the superpowers, although, of course, the treaty verification mechanism would be open to contributions by all parties.

4. Treaty specificity. Monitoring without an arms control agreement does not constitute verification: verification involves monitoring compliance with explicit arms-control understandings. Moreover, generally speaking, the verification mechanism must be treaty-specific. It should operate only with respect to the agreements to which it expressly applies, as part of an overall verification process for those agreements alone. If a verification mechanism is intended to apply to several agreements, this must be done with the express consent of all the parties involved. The creation of any "third party" mechanism for treaty monitoring should be avoided.

5. Participation in verification. All parties to an agreement should have the option, at least, of participating in the verification mechanisms of that agreement. This does not mean that all parties should have access to data from the purely national means of other parties, when these means are used for verification. It does mean that there is a right of participation in any multilateral verification mechanism set up by a treaty.

The creation of a treaty-specific multilateral verification mechanism has the distinct advantage of allowing for participation by all parties and, consequently, enhancing support for the conclusion of the treaty. Such a mechanism also provides a vehicle for authoritatively collecting verification data and procedures for establishing noncompliance. Finally, it provides a forum for co-operative activity toward a common goal, with the resulting confidence-building this entails.

To include the direct participation of all parties in every aspect of verification activity, however, could result in unworkably complex and cumbersome procedures. In addition, duplicating the capabilities already possessed by some States may be unnecessary and costly. In certain instances, it may therefore be reasonable to delegate major responsibilities for verification to a group of countries which possess significant national means, on a collective basis and on the express understanding that there would be access to verification information by all parties.

6. Use of a combination of verification methods, procedures, and techniques. Verification is a process involving a variety of methods, procedures and techniques that operate together. Each of the elements can complement or reinforce the others in such a way that the total effect of elements acting together is greater than the sum of their effects taken independently. Such synergism enhances the effectiveness of the verification system.

Verification methods may be owned and operated nationally by groups of States participating in the agreement (for example, "alliance technical means" and "plurilateral means") or by all the parties collectively, perhaps through an international body acting on their behalf.

7. Interference in internal affairs and sovereignty. A degree of interference in internal affairs and sovereignty may be necessary if the requirements for adequate verification are to be met. The fact that a particular verification activity involves such interference is not *ipso facto* a legitimate ground for rejecting the activity as unacceptable.

An arms control agreement is essentially a contractual exchange: in return for limiting military options (one kind of interference in internal affairs) greater information about the relevant military activities of potential adversaries will be provided for verification purposes (another kind of interference in internal affairs). The loss of some degree of sovereignty is more than compensated by an increased degree of security.

8. Trade secrets. Verification involves the acquisition of information relevant to military and related activities for the purpose of determining compliance with arms control obligations. Provisions to protect against the possible disclosure of sensitive commercial or economic information obtained during verification activities should be included in the design and operation of any verification system.

9. Negotiating verification provisions. Past negotiating experience has demonstrated the close interrelationships between the elaboration of an agreement as such and the elaboration of verification procedures for that agreement. While no verification system can be finalized before the scope, nature and purpose of the arms control measures of the agreement are known, it is similarly impossible to ascertain this scope, nature and purpose without being aware of the capabilities of the parties to verify the agreement and what verification provisions they are willing to accept. Negotiation of the verification provisions and substantive arms control measures in a treaty should therefore proceed *pari pasu.*

Conclusion

Ten years have passed since the Final Document of the first special session of the General Assembly devoted to disarmament was concluded. While the principles in that Document remain relevant, it is no longer sufficient to repeat what was agreed on ten years ago. We must move on to identify and elaborate upon the positive progress that has to be realized in the interim period. The United Nations has a critical leadership role to play in this context. The importance of this role is underlined by the forthcoming third special session devoted to disarmament, at which progress in developing a new and agreed authoritative statement on principles relating to multilateral verification would be a very significant accomplishment.

SOME PRACTICAL ASPECTS OF ARMS CONTROL VERIFICATION

*Ben Sanders**

This paper discusses some practical and administrative aspects of the verification of measures of arms limitation or disarmament. It draws first on experience gathered within the framework of one particular set of verification measures, namely the so-called safeguards system of the International Atomic Energy Agency (IAEA), by means of which that organization assures itself that nuclear materials and installations are not used for purposes proscribed in the agreements that call for the implementation of those measures. The observations made in this paper derive from developments beginning in the early 1960s, when IAEA first elaborated a simple set of safeguards with respect to research reactors, up to the present, when the Agency's safeguards extend to all stages of the nuclear fuel cycle, including installations handling large amounts of fissionable material in bulk form. The paper attempts to project onto the wider screen of multilateral disarmament verification some of the lessons learned in a quarter of a century of effort to develop a technically feasible and effective safeguards system; in devising and negotiating the diplomatic agreements and administrative arrangements that underlie the deployment of that system; and in the system's practical implementation, both in the States concerned and at its headquarters.

The lessons thus learned may not all be directly applicable to other situations. The situation of IAEA was unique in several respects. Thus, for instance, by the time it was called upon to elaborate and deploy a verification system in respect of important arms limitation measures such as the Treaty on the Non-Proliferation of Nuclear Weapons (NPT) of 1968, and the Treaty on the Denuclearization of Latin America (the Treaty of Tlatelolco) of 1967, it had been in existence for a decade and had an active secretariat, alert to the new questions to be dealt with and ready to act as the senior cadre for a newly expanding staff. Besides giving the Agency a priceless advantage in terms of time gained, the fact that the

---

*Ben Sanders, former Director of the Information and Studies Branch, United Nations Department for Disarmament Affairs, is Head of the Program for Promoting Nuclear Nonproliferation.

new function was housed in an existing organizational entity inevitably put its stamp on the organizational and administrative approaches followed.

Even with those and various other advantages, gearing up for the new task has required a huge effort. In particular, it has become obvious to those responsible for the implementation of the safeguards system on the present large, and still growing, scale that the job presents a multitude of problems besides the purely technical ones. These problems include a wide variety of diplomatic, legal and administrative matters; questions of organization, management and finance; personnel questions including recruitment, training, career issues, outposting, working conditions, and remuneration—each of which may have a bearing on the way the job is done and thus eventually on the quality of the verification.

It is obviously not possible to deal with all the issues likely to arise in devising and deploying a new set of verification measures and in creating the necessary organizational base for that deployment. This paper highlights only a few aspects of the subject. In particular, no attempt is made here to sketch a coherent picture of the type of organization that might be involved. Inevitably, that organization will be a highly complicated structure having many technical, political and administrative components, ingeniously conceived to serve its purpose to the best effect but always constrained in practice by political reality, economic limitations and bureaucratic expediency. Given the many variables that figure in the development of any international verification system, attempting to predict the administrative and institutional detail of such a system necessarily involves an unconscionable amount of speculation. But if there is a single immutable lesson to be drawn from one's experience in a world of political uncertainties, it is that in order to be viable, an international verification system must not only be equipped with the technical means to ensure that the provisions of the pertinent agreement are complied with: it should also be endowed with a high degree of immunity to the many factors that will work against its efficacy. This immunity can exist only if the system has good people to work it, and the right structural framework for those people to work in.

Literally, "verification" means "to make sure of the truth"; in arms limitation parlance it generally refers to the process followed to make certain that parties to an agreement comply with its terms. With respect to the parties to which it is applied, verification should help ensure that they continue to behave in the way they have bound themselves to behave and should serve to prevent them from breaking the promise they made by entering into the agreement. With regard to the other parties, verification should give them the confidence that their treaty partners adhere to the rules, or, conversely, should give them timely warning of a breach of that promise and permit them to react appropriately. Since all parties to the agreement are subject to the verification process, these aspects of deterrence, of confidence building and of timely warning are valid for each of them. They are inseparable parts of the concept of verification and each should be given due attention in the verification system. They reinforce one another and together add to the viability of the agreement of which they form a part. Obviously, the way in which the verification is implemented, and the entity responsible for its implementation, will play a very important part in the establishment and maintenance of confidence among the parties to the agreement and in the promotion of the security that is its ultimate aim.

The object of verification is to make sure that the specific purposes of the agreement are realized and that particular things are done or not done. The experience gained in the development and application of the several IAEA safeguards systems quite clearly illustrates how each arms-limitation agreement may serve a specific purpose and how the object of verification, hence its nature, can differ from agreement to agreement.[1] The nature of verification must depend on the purpose of the agreement.

The assurance of compliance with a measure of disarmament or arms limitation is meant to serve the security of the parties who divest themselves of, or limit, the means of warfare concerned. States that do not have such means obtain through verification the confidence that permits them to forgo obtaining them or acquiring alternative means of warfare. For the disarmers, verification is a vital element of security; for the "nonarmers," it is principally a confidence-building factor that assists them in staying unarmed.

The Verification Body

It follows that for agreements imposing multilateral obligations, international means of verification are needed. In order to be credible to the parties to the agreement, such means will have to be developed, deployed, managed and implemented by those parties. As a rule, the parties cannot provide them individually, both because they lack the means and because one-sided findings of compliance or noncompliance would lack credibility. Parties will therefore tend to entrust this function to a common body over which they exercise a measure of control.

The international verification function presumes the existence of a competent and well-equipped organizational entity to serve as its base of operations. On political and practical grounds it may be desirable (or unavoidable) for a future organization established to monitor compliance with multilateral arms control agreements to be associated with an existing multilateral institution. For the sake of efficiency and technical autonomy it is very important that the organization should not be subsidiary to the body with which it is so associated. It may be recalled that IAEA, which reports annually to the United Nations General Assembly, is not subsidiary to the United Nations. It is an autonomous body; neither a specialized agency nor a branch of the United Nations. To retain its autonomy, any verification organization should be so conceived as to avoid the veto of a superior political organ, the irrelevance of a multilateral gathering preoccupied with political utterances and the infiltration of its governing organs and of its secretariat by considerations, practices and processes not immediately germane to its technical purposes and its practical operation. It should be exclusively concerned with the technical and logistical aspects of verification and with the analysis of the data obtained and should be free to function with a minimum of political disturbance.

Should the international community decide to create one body for the verification of compliance with several multilateral measures of arms limitation or disarmament, then it would seem appropriate that each area of verification should be funded separately by the parties to the agreement concerned; only general overhead costs would be common items and the over-all supervision of its management might be entrusted to an executive council that could take its decisions either by consensus or through a process of weighted voting, based on each State's involvement in various arms-control measures under its jurisdiction. The organization could report to the multilateral negotiating and deliberating bodies directly involved, but it should derive its mandates only from the pertinent agreements and from review or other relevant conferences.

Legal Bases for Verification

Most verification functions are highly technical in nature. It is cumbersome to lay down in the basic agreement every aspect of its implementation. This requires various layers of executive subagreements of which some may be worked out between the parties to the agreement, others may have to be so detailed and specific that it is not practical to do so in the general terms in which any convention, no matter how refined, will be couched. The elaboration of such subagreements must be left to the body entrusted with the verification task and will become a subject of individual negotiation between that body and each of the States involved. This entails the risk that the implementation of the verification function may vary from place to place and from situation to situation, and great pains have to be taken to avoid any such dissimilarity in treatment.

The 1968 Treaty on the Non-Proliferation of Nuclear Weapons is a case in point. The Treaty itself does not contain verification provisions: it merely obligates nonnuclear weapon States party to it to conclude agreements with IAEA (the international body singled out in the Treaty to apply the required verification measures) and it gives some general indications of the purpose of the verification measures ("safeguards") to be applied, the items to which they shall apply and the manner in which they are to be implemented. The Statute of IAEA empowers that body to apply safeguards and indicates what they shall consist of; it also sets out sanctions for the case of non-compliance with a safeguards agreement. This in itself is not enough: in order to be able to fulfil the verification function allotted to it in the NPT, the Agency has developed a standard safeguards agreement, which contains the major provision of the system of safeguards applied by the Agency with respect to the nuclear activities of each of the parties.

The Treaty contains the basic layer of obligations; the standard safeguards agreement is the second layer. But detailed though it may be, the safeguards agreement cannot contain the many administrative and technical rules which determine how precisely the respective rights and obligations of the State and the Agency are realized. Those rules, which pertain to all safeguards operations in the State, are laid down in so-called subsidiary arrangements. These prescribe, for instance, the nature and frequency of the State's periodic material accountancy reports and the way in which the Agency shall carry out its inventories of various categories of nuclear material. And even this is not enough. On top of this third layer of largely logistical understanding, there is a fourth level of agreement: the facility attachment, which is concluded for each of the installations under safeguards, and which specify the actual safeguards procedures to be applied, given the exact technical nature and peculiarities of the plant in question.

It should be obvious that to avoid anomalies and inequities in the application of this four-tiered system, painstakingly negotiated with each of the parties to the NPT (or at least those with nuclear energy programs), the implementing body must make a great effort at uniformity. Experience shows that in such negotiations, each State seeks a most-favoured-nation treatment. But States naturally compare notes on the treatment they receive. The obvious result is that any concession made, any weakness shown, any exception granted by the verifying organization will be a precedent for all other similar actions: the moment one State receives favourable treatment, all others will expect to be treated the same way. Thus the verification system is subject to an unremitting process of dilution, which only a body of strong and more or less autonomous international standing can effectively fight. The more politicized the verifying authority, the less effective is the verification.

One notes that the Treaty on the Elimination of Intermediate-Range and Shorter-Range Missiles (the INF Treaty) represents an attempt to include in a single set of documents the basic obligations of the parties, a description of the way in which those obligations are to be met, detailed provisions for the verification of compliance with the treaty, as well as rules and procedures for the on-site inspections which are part of the verification system. This is, I believe, the first time that parties to an arms limitation agreement of this degree of technical complexity have sought to regulate in one layered set of texts not only the way in which they aim to live up to that agreement but the precise means by which they intend to check on its compliance, down to the tiniest administrative and technical detail. This approach would seem to have both advantages and disadvantages. It must have greatly complicated the negotiations and it may make the ratification procedure more difficult than it might otherwise have been. On the other hand, it may help prevent some later misunderstanding between the parties on the means of implementation of the verification provisions and it will go far to defeat the arguments of those who have criticized the Treaty on the grounds that it does not make adequate provision for on-site verification.

One wonders, however, if even at this level of detail it is possible to provide for all eventualities and it may be feared that an approach of this kind, which is in any case not certain to prevent all later misunderstandings, may entail a degree of rigidity that could hamper rather than facilitate implementation. Then, again, one should realize that in a bilateral agreement of this kind parties keep each other in balance and are in a position to take countermeasures upon the mere suspicion that the other side is cheating. Multilateral disarmament conventions may not readily lend themselves to such an all-at-once approach, if only because the negotiations would be immensely complicated. It further remains to be seen if this approach could be applicable also in the case of an agreement banning the production of certain arms or warfare agents (such as a chemical weapons convention), providing for the application of measures of verification at production facilities. Most likely, in such cases a multi-tiered system like the one employed by IAEA pursuant to the NPT, involving the specification of verification practices for each factory, would be unavoidable.

The establishment of procedures to verify compliance with multilateral agreements for arms limitation or disarmament—on which this paper focuses—may both be easier and more difficult than it is with regard to bilateral agreements. Multilateral agreements such as a chemical weapons ban will probably have many parties. That fact is likely to deter stand-out States from negotiating too unreasonably for far-reaching constraints on verification, lest they lose credibility. But practice teaches that a concession once granted to one State becomes law as far as all the others are concerned and if one nation can set itself up as the champion defending all others against the onslaught of the "big, bad verification wolf" it may well succeed in weakening the procedures beyond a reasonable level. As we have seen in NPT safeguards practice, a State that is beyond reproach from a nuclear proliferation point of view and is traditionally known for its pro-arms-limitation attitudes may yet be quite capable of forcing the verifying body to accept changes in its system that are liable to do real harm to the integrity and efficacy of its operation. This fact in itself would seem to indicate that the verifying organization will need every bit of political autonomy and strength it can muster.

Inspection Management

If it is a basic requirement for the potential efficacy of the verification system that it rely on a solid basis, it is equally important that it should be intelligently applied and managed and that the human resources on which its operation depends should be of first-rate quality. The management of a verification system presumes a level of intellectual and political independence and objectivity which is hard to find in every-day life but which is a *sine qua non* in the establishment of confidence in an international framework. The inspectors who apply the system in the field should not only be capable of operating independently, often under adverse and disagreeable conditions, but they should be endowed with tact, patience, technical competence, energy and stamina, a gift for languages, courage and honesty and, above all, should be convinced of the importance of their jobs. Surprisingly, it is possible to find such people, or it has been so in the past. It is an open question, however, how long it will remain possible to find them and especially whether, with several agreements in place requiring verification, and a growing number of installations to be inspected, one will be able to find the large number of people needed for the job—not only now, but for the indefinite future.

The present international civil servant—once considered a privileged figure—has come to realize that international life may hold more disadvantages than does the easier existence of the national bureaucrat or the industrial employee whose remuneration grows with his performance. Nuclear industry is going through a slump and for the moment the job of nuclear inspector may offer some rewards hard to find in private life. This does not apply to the same degree for the chemical industry, for instance, and to be capable of acting as inspector under a treaty banning the production of chemical warfare agents a person must command a level of expertise likely to be more highly rewarded in private industry than in an international organization, where, moreover, the work may be less interesting and career prospects uncertain—not to dwell on the problems associated with life in a foreign country: problems of schooling, housing, language and many more, among which often the most important is that of the working spouse unable to find a suitable occupation abroad.[2]

This leads to two conclusions right away. First, any verification body should be in a position to offer candidates for inspectors' jobs good employment conditions. Second, the inspection task should be so circumscribed as to be capable of being carried out by persons of average intelligence and training. The latter will be a function of careful development and prudent management. The inspector should be instructed as to precisely what data should be obtained and how, and the system should be so designed as to make this data-gathering relatively easy. To the extent possible—and this is a third and fundamental conclusion—data should be interpreted by a managerial apparatus responsive to very high demands for objectivity and technical competence and endowed with a great measure of functional independence in its analytical tasks. These requirements are well illustrated in various working documents generated in various subgroups of the Conference on Disarmament, which reflect the importance the negotiators in Geneva attach to this aspect of verification. But, while such negotiations should set the stage for the establishment of a verification body and give it all the power it needs to work, the efficacy of its operation is determined by the quality of the people running it. In the end, the viability and credibility of a verification organization will depend on the quality of the personnel it can attract.

But verification is not based exclusively, or even primarily, on on-site inspection and the analysis of its results. Where it involves production processes that handle bulk materials, for instance, such as chemicals or nuclear substances, an overall analysis of compliance must take account, *inter alia,* of the characteristics of the installations covered, as reflected in the design information to be presented; the results of checks on quantitative and qualitative bookkeeping data with respect to the material produced, received and shipped out; investigations of plant management's records on the operation of the installations concerned, and on throughput, transfers and receipts and of any potentially relevant incident. Among the various aspects of verification, inspection is only one of many jobs, albeit usually the most visible and often the most difficult one. The managerial and analytical functions involved go far beyond the complexities engendered by on-site inspection.

Concluding Comments

Multilateral verification of arms control agreements is a new phenomenon in international affairs. It is a novelty, not only because it has introduced technical complexities that few diplomats have been traditionally equipped to handle, but because it represents a fundamental departure from the principle of sovereignty of nation-States. International verification implies the involvement of the world community in the affairs of the individual State. However much a State is determined to live up to its international obligations, it will tend to find it politically and psychologically difficult to accept the concept that under most arms control agreements it must prove its innocence to be believed. It is all the more difficult for the State to have to supply part of this proof by submitting to the alien intrusion inherent in most verification systems.

The structure of the verification agency must take account of this reality and be responsive to it. It must be able to carry out a highly complicated technical task, under difficult political and practical conditions. It must meet unique organizational and managerial requirements in the way it is set up, and it must operate at a level of technical competence high enough to permit the international community to give full credence to its findings. Above all, it must have the right people and the means to attract and keep them and make the best use of them.

There is no need to point out the importance of disarmament and arms limitation in international security. Verification is generally recognized as an essential element in present-day disarmament measures. The logistical and administrative problems involved in the establishment of a viable and convincing system of verification are less widely known. Many of those are so down-to-earth as to appear too pedestrian and trivial for serious consideration in deliberations dealing with subjects of immediate significance for the security of the parties involved.

This paper is an attempt to show that the practical and pedestrian aspects of verification must be faced, lest the system be unable to operate effectively and thus frustrate the very purpose of the disarmament agreement it is meant to support.[3] There is an old fable about a string of causes and effects, from quite trivial to enormously important: starting with the loss of a nail, via the consequent casting of a horseshoe, the resulting lameness of the horse, preventing the rider from delivering his message in time so that the army's commander lacked the data that would have helped him win the battle—and eventually leading to the fall of an entire kingdom. It should never be said that a lack of readiness to deal with the apparent trivia of verification practice made effective disarmament impossible—at the eventual expense of world peace and security.

Notes

1. For example: The Statute of IAEA forbids the use of Agency-supplied nuclear items "for any military purpose". The pertinent agreements therefore make provision for the application of safeguards designed to allow the Agency to assure itself that its assistance is used exclusively for peaceful purposes. The agreements concluded by the Agency pursuant to the NPT, on the other hand, contain provision for the application of safeguards to ensure that the State concerned abides by its undertaking not to develop or manufacture nuclear weapons or any other nuclear explosive device. The NPT does not prohibit the use of nuclear material for nonexplosive military purposes, such as the propulsion of naval vessels, and the safeguards system developed for application under the Treaty takes account of this fact. Thus the two categories of agreement have distinct purposes; in conse-

quence, the respective verification systems have different objects; and the nature of the verification differs accordingly.

2. The question of the political independence of the international inspector is both very important and extremely sensitive. However objective and impartial one is in one's professional approach, one's background tends to influence one's judgment. This involuntary bias may be offset where appropriate by careful balancing of inspection teams, for instance. If it is too strong, however, it may put the impartiality of the verification exercise at risk. The average international official will naturally maintain some form of contact with his or her home country and its authorities but it is essential that he or she should retain a high degree of independence with respect to those authorities. The shorter the term of employment of the inspector, the harder it will be to maintain that independence, in view of the necessity of going back home in the near future and resuming a career. The inspector would therefore tend to stay "on the right side of the authorities" and for the sake of the future might even have to comply with requests for services that might not generally be considered to be in accordance with the duties of a loyal international civil servant. Conversely, if the international official may have confidence that the organization offers real career possibilities, adequate remuneration, job satisfaction, timely promotion and all the many other considerations that together make it worth one's while to identify oneself with it, the issue of independence would tend to play less of a role. However, practice shows that career jobs are becoming more scarce in most international organizations and that it is in fact the policy of a growing number of international organizations (including IAEA!) to offer only short-term appointments. This is an issue which will have to be faced.

3. One aspect that should be faced concerns *timing*. The establishment of a verification system is very time-consuming. Again, taking IAEA as an example, it involves the development, elaboration and codification of a set of technical measures and procedures, the recruitment and training of inspectors and headquarters personnel to operate the system, the negotiation of agreements and administrative arrangements with States and possibly also with facility operators within those States, to furnish the practical conditions of implementation. Moreover, while IAEA already existed at the time the agreements to be verified by it were concluded, there is at present no other international body to which the verification function of further arms control agreements can be immediately entrusted. Thus, in addition to the points listed, the organizational question— which may well be one of the most difficult among a formidable list of issues—will also have to be faced. And it will have to be faced early. One problem is that as soon as an arms-limitation or disarmament agreement is concluded, parties whose security significantly benefits from its implementation will seek to put it into effect. However, it will be difficult in practice to obtain funds for the creation of a verification apparatus before the pertinent agreement has been concluded and has entered into force. This consideration might be an argument in

favour of the creation of a single verification body for all or most arms-limitation agreements, even before any further agreements have been concluded. However, even if such a body existed, it would most likely be unable to obtain the funds necessary to prepare and commence operations pursuant to any impending agreement until after that agreement had actually entered into force.

OPENNESS, TRANSPARENCY, AND CONFIDENCE-BUILDING

*Victor L. Issraelyan**

The process of disarmament and its internationalization, together with the gradual evolution of a comprehensive security system through collective efforts, is creating a need to establish confidence and promote *glasnost* in international relations on a wide scale, with a view to setting up a reliable verification mechanism.

We believe that in order to achieve agreements in all areas of disarmament and to implement them successfully it is particularly important to ensure greater openness and predictability in the military sphere, to exchange necessary information, and to establish a system of strict and effective verification of compliance with the obligations assumed by the parties to a treaty.

In the present circumstances, when the groundwork is being laid for the building of a world that is truly nuclear-free, confidence cannot be restricted to selected measures or spheres. It has assumed a completely new dimension, requiring a transition to a broad policy of confidence-building.

Confidence has a special role to play in an area as sensitive as that of disarmament, in which national security interests are directly affected. It is, I believe, here more than anywhere else that confidence must manifest itself in concrete action.

Indeed, what spurs on the arms race is fear and suspicion. At the same time, a very clear trend is emerging, with the arms race becoming self-contained and having its own internal logic and in fact precluding the building up of confidence. The result is a vicious circle, with mistrust generating an arms race and the arms race in turn intensifying suspicion.

The formula, "The more arms, the greater the insecurity and suspicion" should be countered by another: "The more disarmament, the greater the confidence."

The most important instruments of confidence are openness, or *glasnost*. There is no need to prove that where there is a shroud of

---

*Victor L. Issraelyan, former Permanent Representative to the Conference on Disarmament, is professor at the Diplomatic Academy of the Foreign Ministry of the Soviet Union.

mystery, suspicions frequently arise, myths are created and speculation begins. Openness should not however be an end in itself; rather, it should be an instrument for the building of confidence: the goal is not openness and transparency in continuing the arms race. Disarmament measures constitute the shortest road to genuine openness. After all, in disarming we are at the same time opening ourselves up by eliminating those areas of activity that are primarily concerned with secrecy. Openness is intended to remove sources of suspicion and create an atmosphere of clarity and predictability conducive to real disarmament.

There can be no doubt that confidence can rest only upon verifiable knowledge. The Soviet Union, together with its Warsaw Treaty allies, has put forward a far-reaching proposal for consultations with the countries members of the North Atlantic Treaty Organization (NATO) with a view to comparing the military doctrines of the two alliances, analyzing their character and engaging in joint consideration of the direction in which they should evolve in order to dispel the mutual suspicion and mistrust that have been built up over the years, arrive at a better understanding of each other's intentions, and ensure that military thinking and the doctrines of the military blocs and their adherents are based on principles of defence.

We have therefore proposed, in essence, a major measure of confidence and openness that makes it possible to ascertain the sincerity of our intentions and the truly defensive character of both our doctrine and our practice in military matters, and, in turn, makes it possible for us to receive assurances of the sincerity of the statements by leaders of the States members of the North Atlantic Alliance to the effect that they would use military force only in response to aggression.

This is our concrete contribution to a reasonable, responsible, rational organization of international affairs. Standards—unheard of before— are being established with regard to *glasnost* and with regard to the extent of mutual inspection and verification of obligations assumed.

The conclusion of the Treaty on the Elimination of Intermediate-Range and Shorter-Range Missiles has been a major breakthrough in terms of confidence-building and verification. The Treaty provides for as many as six different types of on-site inspection.

For the purpose of launching talks on the reduction of armed forces and conventional armaments in Europe, we propose that data be exchanged in the near future on the armed forces and conventional armaments of the countries in Europe that are members of the Warsaw Treaty and of NATO.

We want our policy to be clear to everyone, and, naturally, we expect an appropriate response. This is precisely what motivates us when we take action to build confidence, for example in the area of compliance with the Treaty on the Limitation of Anti-Ballistic Missile Systems (ABM Treaty), the prohibition of nuclear-weapon tests, and the banning of chemical weapons.

In order to eliminate the source of suspicion and to create a healthy atmosphere for a detailed discussion of questions related to compliance with the ABM Treaty, the Soviet Union invited a delegation from the United States House of Representatives to visit the radar station in the area of Krasnoyarsk, which had been the subject of so much speculation.

In order to create an atmosphere of confidence, and in the interests of concluding, at an early date, a convention banning chemical weapons, the Soviet side invited the negotiators on chemical weapons to visit the Soviet military facility at Shikhany to see for themselves typical examples of our chemical weapons and the technologies used for their destruction at a mobile unit. Later, experts will also be able to visit the special facility for the destruction of chemical weapons which is under construction in the area of Chapaevsk.

We also are proposing, in the Conference on Disarmament, that full data on chemical weapons stockpiles and production facilities be exchanged on a multilateral basis.

The Soviet Union is on record as having organized—during its moratorium on nuclear explosions—a trip for foreign representatives to the nuclear test site in the area of Semipalatinsk, to enable American scientists to set up special seismic equipment there to carry out on-site verification of the fact that no explosions were being conducted. Further, we agreed to carry out, jointly with the Americans, a calibrating experiment using nonnuclear underground explosions. The progress of the on-site experiment was observed also by a group of American congressmen.

In our view, confidence-building can also be served by introducing *glasnost* with respect to military spending. The repeated attempts made to reduce military budgets have yielded no results because of difficulties with regard to comparisons. Obviously, we must be fair in comparing defence expenditures, and this is no simple matter since there is a fundamental difference in the price structure of armaments and in the pricing mechanisms of various countries. Upon completion of a radical pricing reform that is to be carried out in our country, we think it will be possible to make a realistic comparison of overall military spending. We believe that in the next two or three years we shall be able to compare data of interest both to us and to our partners, data that would reflect expenditures by the two sides in a uniform way. This is a very serious and responsible undertaking but we are prepared to carry it out.

It is quite clear that the nature of relations makes it impossible simply to decree confidence or to ensure the instantaneous removal of suspicions that have accumulated over many years. For that reason, as we make progress toward the reduction and elimination of certain classes of weapons and the limitation of military potential to a level of reasonable sufficiency, verification will evolve into the most important factor in the attainment of security.

Our position on verification matters is based on the premise that at all stages of disarmament everyone must be completely certain that there will be scrupulous compliance with the agreements undertaken. We favor the most rigorous verification.

IS THERE A GAP BETWEEN ADVANCES IN TECHNOLOGY AND THE ABILITY TO VERIFY?

*Lynn M. Hansen**

Despite the ease with which we speak of verification, it is not a simple subject. Despite all the expertise that currently exists in dealing with it, verification of arms reduction agreements is not a perfect science. Many attempts have been made to define verification and what its role should be in regulating international security. Nevertheless, verification still remains undefined, dependent to a large extent on the political moment, the analysis of threat to the security and well-being of a particular State or group of States. Thus, it is impossible to speak of any agreement as being 100 percent verifiable.

What this means is that arms reduction and the attendant questions of verification—however useful and desirable—will not ensure international peace and stability. Armed forces will not become obsolete merely because agreements have been made and will be made in the future. In pursuing arms control we are like the physician who treats the symptoms of a disease, not the disease itself. If we are to pursue lasting peace and stability, we must seek greater co-operation and understanding across the entire spectrum of human existence. Armaments exist because suspicion and anxiety exist.

As nations attempt to agree to reduce arms, they must agree to tackle the root causes of the existence of arms. The resolution of humanitarian problems, the promotion of individual human rights, cooperation in the fields of ecology, the environment, information and culture, *inter alia,* must progress as part of an overarching political process and thereby contribute to meeting the challenge of a safer, more secure and stable international environment.

This is to say that the reduction and elimination of some categories of armaments is an imperfect process accompanied by increasing problems of verification. The world simply cannot look to this process alone as the solution to problems of world peace.

*Lynn M. Hansen is Assistant Director of the United States Arms Control and Disarmament Agency. The views expressed in this paper are those of the author.

"Is there a growing gap between advances in technologies applicable for military use and verification capabilities?" The short answer is, yes. Verification will become increasingly complex as one moves to further agreements that attempt to deal with complex technology. This paper will attempt to demonstrate this evolution of complexity through a brief consideration of two agreements, the Stockholm Document and the United States-USSR Treaty on the Elimination of Their Intermediate-Range and Shorter-Range Missiles (INF), both of which contain verification provisions, followed by a consideration of two potential agreements, one involving a 50 percent reduction of strategic arsenals, and the other on a comprehensive ban on chemical weapons.

The Stockholm Document

Not even a treaty, but rather a politically binding agreement, the Stockholm Document places each of the 35 States that participate in the Conference on Security and Co-operation in Europe (CSCE) under an obligation to provide certain kinds of information on military activities in Europe involving more than 13,000 troops or 300 tanks and to provide for the observation, by all other participating States, of those activities involving at least 17,000 troops. Further, each State provides an annual calendar listing such notifiable and observable events and reaffirms its obligation undertaken under the Charter of the United Nations not to use or threaten to use force. Exercises above a certain level must be notified two years in advance. More important for our discussion of verification, the Stockholm Document includes the right of any participating State to conduct an on-site inspection of military activities or suspected military activities which incite doubts about compliance with the undertakings in the document.

The objective of verification is to ensure that military activities which routinely occur in Europe are properly notified, observed, and conducted. Other than counting tanks and observing certain categories of military equipment, military technology is not limited by the Stockholm Document, nor are military capabilities in any way circumscribed.

This makes verification, although not an absolutely simple affair, relatively straightforward. Several on-site inspections have already taken place in States belonging to the Warsaw Treaty Organization as well as in States participating in the North Atlantic Alliance. Verification itself has become an almost routine form of confidence-building that supplements the confidence- and security-building measures being implemented.

The INF Agreement

The INF Treaty, on the other hand, is infinitely more complex than the Stockholm Document. It is a historic undertaking both because of its objective—the complete elimination of an entire class of United States and Soviet nuclear missiles—and because of the innovative character and scope of its verification provisions.

The INF Treaty obligates the United States and the Soviet Union to eliminate all their ground-launched ballistic and cruise missile systems having a range capability between 500 and 5,500 kilometers. Weapons systems, that is, military technology, will be destroyed. Consequently, each side will have the right to carry out verification measures to monitor compliance with the Treaty.

The Treaty specifically names the missile systems and the missile-related facilities to be eliminated. It categorizes them as deployed or non-deployed and further defines systems by range. After the treaty enters into force, neither side may produce or flight-test any of the missiles in question. Launchers for prohibited missiles may not be produced.

Up to 100 missiles may be launched within the first six months after the Treaty enters into force for the sole purpose of destroying them. The Treaty provides for the right of each party to establish a system of resident inspectors, up to 30 persons, on the other's territory to continuously monitor a missile-related facility.

The focus of the INF verification system is a declared—that is, overt—inventory of missile systems. This inventory is controlled by specific geographical and movement constraints based on a partitioning of the territories of the two States into limited areas where INF missile systems are allowed, and a larger residual area where they are prohibited unless they are notified as being in transit.

The verification régime in its entirety is designed both to control the declared overt INF inventory and to make as complicated and costly as possible the acquisition of any covert, illegal inventory.

To summarize, eight key verification elements characterize the INF Treaty:

1. Production and test ban.
2. Continuous monitoring of an INF-related facility, including portal monitoring and perimeter patrol.
3. Restriction of missiles and launchers to designated facilities and areas.
4. Designation of deployment areas and containment areas (corrals).
5. Transit notification.
6. Baseline inspection.
7. Elimination procedures.
8. Short-notice inspection of active missile support facilities and operating bases.

Paradoxically, the INF Treaty is at once extraordinarily complex and remarkably simple. Its complexity is reflected in the number and nature of the verification provisions it incorporates and in the volume and level of technical detail it contains.

The simplicity of the Treaty is evident from a number of relevant factors:

1. It is a bilateral agreement involving only two states directly with appropriate consultations among allies.
2. It seeks to eliminate an entire class of weapons.
3. The weapons to be eliminated, while technologically sophisticated, are produced exclusively to meet military requirements.
4. Their production, storage, transfer, testing and training use are at all times under military oversight: there is no mistaking the intended use or purpose of a nuclear-armed missile.
5. The on-site inspection provisions are accessible only to the two parties to the Treaty.
6. One principal provision, the ban on all flight-testing of intermediate-range missiles, can be monitored by the national technical means under the control of each party.

Each of these simplicity factors contributes significantly to making the arduous task of verifying compliance with the Treaty more manageable. Every deviation from a simplicity factor makes verification a far more challenging and daunting task. And the more sophisticated and varied the technology involved, the more difficult verification will be.

In the introduction to this paper, the short answer to the question posed was yes: there is a growing gap between advances in technologies with possible military application and the capability of verifying arms reduction or elimination agreements involving such technologies. This is not to say that such agreements should not be pursued—for indeed they should—but only to provide an approach to answering a provocative question. Two examples, that of a possible START agreement covering a 50 percent reduction in strategic nuclear armaments and the negotiations on a comprehensive ban on chemical weapons, will be used as illustrative examples in support of the affirmative answer to the question posed.

Strategic Arms Reduction

In the proposed agreement on strategic arms reduction (START), as in the INF Treaty, the object of the negotiations is a bilateral agreement to reduce and limit strategic nuclear missile systems. As in the INF Treaty, the weapons involved are produced, stored, transferred and tested exclusively under military oversight. And, again as in the INF Treaty, implementation affects essentially only the two states parties to the treaty with the verification provisions accessible only to the two parties which have a direct stake in the agreement.

There are, however, also major differences. One critical difference is that the proposed treaty will relate to arms reduction. Another is that differing technologies must be taken into account, that is, ground-launched systems, sea-launched systems, and systems that involve manned aircraft. Some ground-launched systems are located at fixed, permanent sites; others are mobile. Sea-launched systems involve submarines, which are widely dispersed, mobile and difficult to detect. Air-launched systems may include such diverse munitions as gravity bombs and a variety of guided missiles including air-launched cruise missiles. Already, the verification problem has become more complex.

Let us focus on one aspect of this complexity. START will be an arms reduction treaty allowing each side to retain large numbers of strategic missiles. It follows that each party will retain the need for flight-testing and production. Whereas in the INF Treaty the ban on flight-testing would help, over time, to provide confidence that neither side was keeping a prohibited capability, this mechanism will be absent in a treaty on strategic arms reduction.

Under the INF Treaty, observation of a single missile outside an allowed region, not in announced transit, would suffice to determine that a party was in violation of the terms of the Treaty. Indeed, at the end of the destruction process, mere possession could serve the same purpose. In START, because the sides will be allowed to keep large numbers of weapons, determination of compliance (that is, verification) will require evaluating the status of observed weapons—remember the various categories: land, sea, and air—in their relationship to all others which the party is allowed by treaty to possess.

In addition to dealing with the complexity arising from negotiation of reductions as opposed to elimination, the START negotiations aim to limit strategic capability by defining limits on strategic offensive delivery systems, warheads, nuclear armament of heavy bombers, and the aggregate throw-weight of intercontinental ballistic missiles (ICBMs) and sea-launched ballistic missiles (SLBMs). Reaching agreement on the definitions and counting rules for these limitations as well as determining procedures for identifying nuclear as opposed to conventional systems is a challenging, complicated process.

All these factors, and possibly others, make each party's national technical means less useful, less definitive than normally assumed. It is clear that verification of a treaty on strategic arms reduction will require even more comprehensive and intrusive measures and means to monitor compliance than does the INF Treaty, which itself set new standards for comprehensive verification.

Because START is a bilateral undertaking with each side committed to a 50 percent reduction in its strategic arsenal, the necessary and intrusive verification measures can probably be agreed on and implemented, albeit with some difficulty.

Chemical Weapons

The 40-nation Geneva Conference on Disarmament is currently negotiating the text of an agreement which, on its entry into force, would constitute a comprehensive global ban on chemical weapons. The multilateral nature of this endeavor, both proper and necessary, distinguishes it from both INF and START, but at the same time makes it more analogous to the Stockholm Document.

The analogy with the Stockholm Document, however, ends at the point where it began: both are multilateral undertakings. The Stockholm Document was regional in nature and did not seek to destroy or limit any military capability. The negotiations on chemical weapons, on the other hand, are global in scale and seek the absolute abolition of all toxic chemical agents that could be used in warfare.

Chemical weapons, unlike nuclear missiles, need not be technologically sophisticated. They are accessible to virtually any country with a capable chemical industry. Unlike the negotiations on nuclear armaments, which relate to weapons produced exclusively for military use, the negotiations on banning chemical weapons must take account of the fact that chemical agents and their precursor chemicals can be manufactured in the commercial chemical industry for legitimate civilian use, for example, in pesticides and pharmaceutical products.

A truly global ban on chemical weapons would affect not only the 40 nations directly involved in the negotiations on the ban but all states capable of producing such weapons. Participation in the verification provisions, including on-site inspection, would need to be available to many different States each having its own stake in the effective implementation of the convention adopted. Other than the objective—that of a comprehensive global ban—there is little simplicity in the negotiation of a convention on chemical weapons.

Under the INF Treaty, the systems to be destroyed are discrete, countable and relatively well-defined. In strategic arms reduction, there is perhaps less precision but nevertheless a clear indication of what is to be covered by a treaty. The technology of chemical agents is of another character. Agents may be referred to by their chemical identity, but are characterized in the negotiations by their toxicity. Everyone has some grasp of the lethal nature of nuclear weapons, but chemical weapons need not be lethal; they may, for example, be any one of several different kinds of incapacitants. In any case, chemicals meeting the toxicity criteria, particularly for precursors, are routinely produced in the civilian commercial chemical industry. The negotiations, including verification issues, must take into account the production of such chemicals for industrial, agricultural, research, medical/pharmaceutical, and law enforcement purposes. Moreover, provisions must be agreed on which allow research for defensive purposes.

Strict verification would need to deal with the requirement to demonstrate that a quantity of toxic chemical was produced for peaceful purposes or would have to face the assumption that it constituted a violation of the proposed convention on chemical weapons.

National technical means such as satellite monitoring will have far less relevance in ascertaining compliance with a ban on chemical weapons than in the agreements involving nuclear missiles. Moreover, such means will not be available to all parties. An effective verification mechanism for a ban on chemical weapons will simply require a degree of inspection of even greater scope and intrusiveness than either INF or the proposed treaty on strategic arms reduction.

Inspections will be required, not only in the United States and the Soviet Union, but for all States possessing the capability of producing chemical weapons; such inspections will not be confined to facilities under military oversight but to a significant proportion of the commercial chemical industry as well.

The recent use of chemical weapons in contravention of the 1925 Geneva Protocol must also be condemned and halted. States need to assume greater individual responsibility for stemming the flow of precursor chemicals that contribute to the proliferation of chemical weapons. The logic of a global ban indicates also the requirement to bring States capable of waging chemical warfare into the convention.

Because inspections will affect both military and civilian facilities and since inspections will be conducted by teams of international inspectors, it will be necessary to establish procedures that protect both sensitive security information and proprietary commercial rights. This basic requirement still needs much consideration since it must be carefully balanced against the need for effective verification.

The size of the international chemical industry alone makes it possible to produce prohibited agents with little fear of discovery. Moreover, this problem is magnified by the element of time. Given 48 hours of warning prior to the arrival of an inspection team, almost any chemical plant could clean up evidence of illicit chemicals, although it might prove more difficult to remove the indications of a production capability. Nevertheless, there would be no "smoking gun," which seems to be an absolute requirement for ascertaining non-compliance.

On-site inspection will therefore need help from technology if it is to be a credible means of verification. Various technologies have been explored in this context but as of now there appears to be nothing that would meet the requirements of being portable, rugged and effective. Because of the need for greater sophistication in dealing with possibly minute traces of prohibited chemicals, more will be demanded of the technology than appears to be currently available.

It would, however, be inaccurate to say that nothing has been done. Finland, the Netherlands, Norway, Sweden, the United Kingdom of Great Britain and Northern Ireland, and the United States of America have all done preliminary work in regard to such technologies as spectroscopy and chromatography. A great deal of work needs to be accomplished, however, with greater focus on the requirements of verifying the non-production of forbidden substances in an operating chemical plant. More potential signatories to a convention on chemical weapons need to concern themselves with this problem. It would be useful to have some insights into what technologies are being investigated in the Soviet Union and other States.

Despite the potential for advanced technology to assist in the verification process, including on-site inspection, it would be folly to assume that the right to conduct challenge inspections will solve the chemical weapons verification problem. In a generic sense, it is neither chemical weapons technology itself nor the lack of sufficient verification that constitutes the problem: rather, it is the sheer complexity and magnitude of the task.

An issue is emerging—a separate one perhaps, but one that is still closely related—in which advances in technology clearly outstrip the ability to verify. This is the area of biochemistry and genetic engineering, in which scientists have been able to achieve near miracles in probing and manipulating the secrets of life. No one should want to impede such work, which seeks to overcome sickness, disease, and the deficiencies of nature, but the potential for misuse also deserves recognition.

Conclusions

First, it should be clear that a great deal of very difficult work remains to be done. In the negotiating environment, one must move from achieving agreements in principle, which exist but do not solve the problems, to achieving agreement by all participants on the myriad of details that must be taken into account.

Second, it is easier to obtain agreement on necessary details when the technological issues are relatively simple and straightforward; a corollary is that agreement will become more difficult as the number of states participating increases.

Third, the verification process is far from perfect. Indeed, in some cases the difficulty of the undertaking is of such magnitude that it is not yet possible fully to comprehend how to resolve the problems. Here technological innovation may be required to assist in the process.

Fourth, it is essential to achieve and maintain a stable strategic balance, both on a global scale and on a regional basis; stability and a balance of forces at lower levels must be the immediate objective.

Fifth, whereas openness, transparency, and political acceptance of on-site inspection are necessary in dealing with the basic issue of verification, more must be done to deal with the root causes of the existence of arms: otherwise, negotiations run the risk of foundering on the iceberg of suspicion.

THE GAP BETWEEN ADVANCES IN WEAPON SYSTEMS AND VERIFICATION CAPABILITIES

*Hubert Thielicke**

Verification measures play an important part in creating the confidence necessary for the functioning of disarmament agreements and in ensuring that such agreements are observed by all the parties. In the disarmament process, verification will become one of the most important means of guaranteeing security. Agreements on arms limitation and disarmament should therefore provide for appropriate and effective verification measures. These may include national measures (e.g., as national monitoring systems and national technical means) and international measures (e.g., exchange of data, international organs, and on-site inspections).

Not only is there an arms race between States and groups of States; there is also fierce competition between weapons technology, in which there are rapid advances, and the verification capabilities. Most scientific experts agree that the gap between the two is increasing. Only a few of the experts, however, seem to be fatalistic in this regard. The experience of the last few decades shows, first, that each new weapon technology has been followed by a counter-technology, and that the means of verification have, to a large extent, caught up with new weapon systems. Second, where the necessary political will was there, agreements were concluded providing for the necessary verification measures.

Nevertheless, today and in the foreseeable future, the rapid use of the latest scientific and technological achievements for military purposes will pose a number of serious problems for negotiators who are seeking effective means of controlling new weapons systems. In this regard, the following questions should be considered:
—What are the tendencies in the relationship between weapons technology and verification capabilities?
—Which solutions might make it possible to control weapons technology in the interests of achieving disarmament and stable international security?

---

*Hubert Thielicke is Head of Section in the Division for United Nations Affairs of the Ministry for Foreign Affairs of the German Democratic Republic.

The Qualitative Arms Race and Technical Verification Capabilities

A special feature of the arms race is the use of science and technology for military purposes, which leads to the rapid succession of weapon systems, their growing sophistication and an immense improvement in their technical parameters. This trend is generally referred to as the "qualitative arms race." To a large extent the qualitative arms race is spurred on by the concept of deterrence. By its inherent logic, deterrence is based on worst-case scenarios. This automatically leads to efforts to achieve superiority and more effective military power. The other side responds in the same way, which leads to ever new rounds in the vicious circle of the qualitative arms race. This is sometimes very closely connected with a kind of "technology fetish," that is, a belief in the ability to solve political problems by technical means. Experience gained from history leads, however, to the following conclusions:

1. There are no technical solutions to political problems.
2. Even the technology that is apparently the most developed is not error-free. Nevertheless, the race for new weapons technology leads to serious problems for disarmament negotiations, in both the political and the technical fields:
   a. The emergence of new technologies is often connected to attempts to preclude limitations for certain categories of weapons (e.g. space weapons), to block negotiations (e.g., implications of the production of binary chemical weapons on chemical weapons negotiations), or even to undermine existing agreements (e.g., ABM Treaty, and the biological weapons Convention)
   b. Advances in weapons technology can complicate the verification of arms limitation and disarmament measures (see below)
   c. There are also increased possibilities for "countermeasures" to avoid surveillance by national technical means (NTM) or other means, ranging from measures to impede verification (e.g., evasion techniques, concealment measures) to weapons directly threatening NTM (e.g., ASAT).

Since the beginning of substantive negotiations on arms limitation and disarmament in the 1960s, there has always been a race between weapons technology and verification capabilities. A case in point is the endeavour to control MIRV (multiple independently targetable re-entry vehicles) technology in the SALT process. With the advances in microelectronics, avionics, microbiology and so forth, this race takes on a new aspect. Scientific experts estimate that weapons technology cannot follow. This applies both to the numbers of weapons and to their characteristics (including range, mission, payload, launcher, deployment). In this regard, the characteristics of emerging weapons are mentioned:

—**Versatility** (e.g. dual-capable and mission-flexible weapons).
—**Concealability** (e.g., miniaturization and micro-miniaturization of system components, sensor deception).
—**Mobility** (e.g., the fact that strategic weapons are becoming increasingly independent of large, complex launch facilities as a result of miniaturization, encapsulation, remote control, and navigation).
—**Diversity** (e.g., the large variety of cruise missile platforms).
—**Quantity** (e.g., the proliferation of nuclear or nuclear-capable weapons, reloadable launchers, and delivery platforms).
—**Testing obscurity** (e.g., tests of missiles at shorter than designed range, much test-work in laboratories, component tests).

All this applies to such weapons systems and weapon-related technologies as cruise missiles, mobile ICBMs, ATBMs, which blur the distinction between ABMs and air defence, ASAT (e.g., F-15 plane), "clip-in" warheads (quickly insertable nuclear components), directed-energy weapons, and stealth technology.

Verification is also made difficult by a certain overlapping between civilian and military technologies. Binary weapons are a case in point. Their chemical components can be produced in civilian chemical enterprises and stored under the guise of "civilian needs." Another gap that also needs to be addressed in the future is that only a few states possess highly sophisticated technical means of verification, whereas there is a growing need for multilateral or even universal disarmament agreements for which a global verification system will be required.

All these trends add to the problems of verification. The problems are further aggravated by opponents of far-reaching disarmament measures. There seems to be a certain "paradox" therein: on the one hand, certain circles which base their security concepts mainly on principles of deterrence are stepping up the qualitative arms race; on the other hand, those are the very circles that then reject far-reaching disarmament measures on the grounds of "a lack of verification." An example in this regard is the report of a commission on an "integrated long-term strategy." The report, which was published in the United States only some days after the beginning of the production of binary weapons, argues *inter alia* against a ban on chemical weapons because it is "not verifiable."

The above-mentioned constraints on verification are mainly of a technical character. To overcome those constraints, a comprehensive approach is needed, one which includes political, technical, economic and other measures.

Enhancing the Efficiency of Technical Means of Verification

Progress in science and technology is constantly bringing about improvements in surveillance techniques. Developments in the field of remote sensing by satellites (e.g., visible light photography, infra-red detection, image-processing, radar) and seismology are the most obvious in this regard. The efficiency of these technical means of verification could be improved by: prohibition of concealment measures, cooperative measures (e.g., counting and type rules), monitoring devices installed within the borders of a party to a treaty (e.g., cameras used by International Atomic Energy Agency (IAEA) inspectors, special seismic stations in nuclear-weapon States with regard to a nuclear test ban), and the protection of NTM (e.g., ASAT ban).

Joint Verification Measures

The limits of surveillance technology—both technical (e.g., the concealability of modern weapons systems) and political (e.g., the possession of NTM by only some countries)—call for verification measures for future agreements that will go far beyond past practices. A point of departure in this regard could be the safeguards system developed and used by IAEA and the verification measures provided for by the Treaty between the United States and the USSR on the Elimination of Their Intermediate-Range and Shorter-Range Missiles.

Thus, future verification systems could include:

1. Procedures for consultation and co-operation to clarify problems in the implementation of agreements.
2. On-site inspections (e.g., systematic and challenge inspections).
3. Procedures for the review and possible readjustment of verification

systems in agreements to possible changes in the technological sphere.
4. Step-by-step multilateralization of national technical means (e.g., an international satellite monitoring agency or international space agency).
5. An international verification organization, which would allow for a comprehensive, integrated approach to verification, universal participation in the verification of compliance with necessary universal agreements, and economy in the use of resources by avoiding the creation of large verification systems for each individual multilateral disarmament measure.

Special Measures of Arms Limitation and Disarmament

Special arms limitation and disarmament measures could be envisaged to curb or prevent developments in weapons technology that would have a long-term negative effect on the disarmament process, including verification capabilities. It is, for example, obvious that complete bans on weapons system rather than numerical limits are preferable from the standpoint of verification.

Such measures could include:

1. Moratoria on the development, production, testing and deployment of certain weapons systems during negotiations.
2. Prohibition of testing (e.g. a comprehensive test ban, prohibition of missile tests).
3. Refraining from the development of new weapons (e.g., new weapon systems based on new physical principles).
4. Prohibition of complete categories of weapons (e.g., chemical weapons, space weapons).

Confidence-Building

The arms race, particularly in its qualitative aspects, is spurred on by suspicion and "worst-case" thinking. More openness in military affairs is necessary to remove the sources of suspicion, to create an atmosphere of clarity and predictability, and to improve the conditions for disarmament. It is therefore necessary to turn from partial measures to a comprehensive policy and strategy of confidence[1] which would also improve the possibilities of verification. Pertinent measures would include:

1. The exchange of information on military activities and weapons and the like, before, during and after the conclusion of agreements.
2. Realistic assessment of the implications of one's own weapon developments for international disarmament negotiations.
3. Joint endeavors by different parties to develop and test effective means of verification, to exchange data and so forth in order to improve the conditions for drawing-up, concluding and implementing disarmament agreements.
4. Military doctrines based on defensive principles, which would exclude the development and creation of weapons for offensive purposes and surprise attack.
5. Agreement on the "military minimum" and "nonoffensive capabilities."

Politico-Economic Means

In order to overcome the economic interests which, in many countries, are connected to the production of new weapons and to ensure a stable, nonreversible disarmament process, there is a need for long-term politico-economic measures. These might include:

1. Conversion of military-oriented scientific and technical installations (e.g., weapons laboratories and other research institutions) into disarmament-oriented facilities (e.g., for the development of verification techniques) and civilian institutions (e.g., in the fields of ecology, energy and food supply);
2. Re-employment of part of the military and research staff as verification personnel in the respective national and international bodies.
3. Creation of national systems to implement disarmament agreements and to guarantee the use of science and technology for peaceful purposes.

There are bound to be manifold problems on the road to comprehensive disarmament guaranteed by effective verification. However, there is no other way to ensure the survival of mankind in the nuclear and space age. It is necessary to break the prevailing trend of producing every weapon system technically possible. This will require a new approach to security, based on the principle that national security cannot be achieved apart from the safety of other States: it can be achieved only on the basis of co-operation.

Note

1. V. Petrovsky, "Confidence and survival of mankind," *Mirowaja Ekonomika i meshdunarodnyie otnoschenija* (Moscow), No. 11/87, pp. 15–26.

Chapter 5

Verification: Underground and Air Monitoring

MULTILATERAL ASPECTS OF THE VERIFICATION OF UNDERGROUND NUCLEAR EXPLOSIONS

*Ola Dahlman**

Bilateral-Multilateral Verification

The present détente between the United States and the USSR has focused world attention on the efforts of the two countries to achieve bilateral arms control and disarmament agreements. The results obtained so far have met with appreciation the world over, and expectations for further, more militarily significant steps are increasing.

The recent United States-USSR Treaty on the Elimination of Their Intermediate-Range and Shorter-Range Missiles (INF Treaty) contains a number of well-specified and detailed bilateral verification provisions, including extensive on-site inspections. These verification provisions clearly demonstrate that today intrusive verification measures can be agreed upon in a bilateral context.

The threshold test-ban Treaty of 1974, which limits permitted nuclear weapon tests to a maximum yield of 150 kilotons, and especially the peaceful nuclear explosions Treaty of 1976, which limits the strength of explosions for civil applications in a similar way, contain extensive verification procedures, which, however, have not been implemented. Efforts, including the conduct of bilateral experiments to calibrate each other's test sites, are now being made to improve the verification procedures of the 1974 Treaty. This is another example of increased readiness on the

*Ola Dahlman is Director of the Swedish National Defence Research Institute.

part of the United States and the Soviet Union to develop extensive bilateral verification measures.

I am convinced that this demonstrated willingness and ability to reach agreement on extensive bilateral verification arrangements as part of bilateral arms control and disarmament treaties are much appreciated around the world. Many may, however, ask what the consequences are for the rest of the world and how it is involved. Limiting the nuclear weapon testing of the United States and the Soviet Union is, for example, not entirely a bilateral United States-USSR affair. Most countries have, by signing the nonproliferation Treaty, renounced their options of developing nuclear weapons and of conducting nuclear weapon tests. All States have a legitimate right and responsibility to verify, according to their needs, that other States also, including the main nuclear weapon States, are halting or limiting their nuclear testing.

Verification to Provide Confidence and Deter Clandestine Activities

A verification system for an arms control agreement has two basic purposes: to provide assurance that other parties to the treaty are respecting their treaty obligations, and to deter parties from violating such obligations. The verification system must therefore provide a high capability for detecting and identifying clandestine activities. It must further limit the risk of creating false alarms by misinterpreting natural events as clandestine activities. A large number of false alarms would rapidly undermine the credibility of the verification system and thus of the treaty itself. This is of especial importance in the case of a test ban treaty, where a large number of earthquakes will be observed and will have to be identified as such.

It is complicated to define the requirements of the verification measures for a particular treaty. The questions of obtaining "adequate" verification have been extensively discussed. In one interpretation offered it was said that "adequate verification satisfies the need of those concerned." This reflects the fact that the verification requirements may differ from one treaty to another and that different countries, for a number of well-founded reasons, may have widely different verification requirements for one and the same treaty. Such different but legitimate verification requirements must be satisfied if the long-term credibility of a treaty is to be maintained. This may require both bilateral and multilateral verification arrangements.

Countries not only have different political reasons for their need for verification of a particular treaty; they also have quite different national technical capabilities for conducting effective monitoring. Some countries may also be in an unfavourable geographical position for obtaining, by national technical means alone, the necessary verification data. International verification arrangements constitute one means of balancing, to some extent, such technical and geographical differences between countries and thus, through international co-operation, providing each country with an acceptable verification capability.

International Verification Measures

In the recent Stockholm Declaration of the sponsors of the Six-Nation Initiative for Peace and Disarmament, the need is recognized for "the establishment of an integrated verification system within the United Nations, as an integral part of a strengthened multilateral framework required to ensure peace and security during the process of disarmament as well as in a nuclear weapon-free world". Such a verification system is likely to contain a number of interrelated components, both political and technical.

The prime purpose of international technical verification measures is to assist States in their national monitoring of a treaty by providing needed information that is not otherwise available. A basic principle is thus that an international verification system should not contain any elements of political judgment, but should rather provide information for political decisions at a national level.

An international verification system can, in principle, contain a number of components that might be described as follows:

1. *On-site observations* can be conducted by human observers or by instruments. These observations are conducted inside the country to be monitored and are primarily aimed at monitoring certain facilities or areas, e.g., test sites and earthquake regions in the case of a test ban. Observations inside the country to be monitored put strong requirements on data authentication and data-transmission security.
2. *Observations as part of a global monitoring system.* Observations are

conducted in many countries and, in principle, outside the country
to be monitored. This reduces the requirements for data authenticity compared to on-site observations. The proposed global seismological monitoring system discussed later and a similar system for
the global monitoring of radioactive fall-out are based on observations provided by participating countries.

3. *System for data transmission.* An essential element in any global and
   regional verification arrangement is a system for the prompt and secure transmission of information from globally or regionally distributed observation sites to participating countries and/or international data centres or organizations.

4. *International data centers,* or corresponding organizations especially established to collect, compile and analyse data provided by
   observers or recording stations. The compiled and preanalyzed data
   are distributed to participating States for their assessment. International data centers should be considered as service facilities for participating States.

Components of an international verification system such as those
listed above can be utilized in the verification of a number of possible future arms control and disarmament treaties. Application of international
verification measures to a nuclear test-ban treaty has been extensively
discussed for more than 30 years, and some of the recent proposals are
discussed below.

A Global Seismological Monitoring System

At the Conference on Disarmament in Geneva, a scientific expert group
has, for a number of years, been working on the design and testing of a
concept of a global seismological monitoring system consisting of the following three components:

1. A global network of at least 50 more or less uniformly distributed,
   highly sensitive seismological stations. These stations would belong
   to the host countries and be operated according to internationally
   agreed rules.

2. An efficient exchange of data on a global scale between participating
   countries and specially established international data centers.

3. International data centers, which would receive and process, ac-

cording to generally agreed procedures, data collected on a global scale. The result of the analysis would be transmitted back to participating countries for national assessment.

The overall purpose of such an international verification system is to assist States parties to a test-ban treaty in their verification by providing pre-analysed data collected on a global scale.

In its work prior to the summer of 1986 the group envisaged a system of fairly heterogeneous stations routinely reporting only preanalyzed data to the international data centers. This was a data exchange very similar to, although faster than, that presently being conducted among scientific institutions.

Agreement has now been reached among the States represented in the group to modernize and considerably upgrade the system technically and also to use all available data in the analysis at the international data centres. This will make the system more complicated, and substantially more data will be exchanged and analysed at the international data centres.

To produce compatible, high-quality data, the expert group has decided to design a modern, standardized station, a "CD station," that could be deployed worldwide and that would produce data directly in computer-readable form.

The exchange of large amounts of data would require an efficient global data-exchange system. Dedicated, high-capacity communication links are to be used to interconnect the international data center. Today such centres are envisaged in Australia, the Soviet Union, Sweden, and the United States. New methods and procedures would have to be developed and established at these centers to analyze the recordings provided by participating stations from each detected seismic signal.

This new system goes far beyond what is available today on a global scale for scientific applications. It is expected to provide more reliable location and depth estimates of detected events. The expected improvement in depth estimation is absolutely essential as the depth of an event is a most efficient parameter for distinguishing between earthquakes, which usually occur at a depth of at least several kilometers, and explosions, which are usually not deeper than one kilometer. It is hoped that it will also reduce the volume of unassociated observations, such as signals detected at one or several stations that cannot definitely be associated with any defined seismic event. The test of an experimental system is due to begin in 1988.

The expert group has not assessed the overall detection and identification capability of such a modernized global system. To be reliable, such estimates have to be based on extensive experimental *matériel* in order to take into account the strong regional variation in the propagation of seismic waves. The problem is further complicated by the variation in the coupling of nuclear explosions into seismic waves between various test sites, an issue that will be studied in the forthcoming bilateral United States-USSR nuclear explosion experiment. In general terms it has, however, been recognized that a global seismological network could have a detection capability corresponding to an explosion of the order of 1 kiloton in hard rock. The capability is limited primarily by prevailing background noise in the Earth and it is not likely that a technical upgrading of the instruments will significantly change the overall detection capability of the global system.

Proposals have been made to put a global seismological monitoring system into routine operation in order to gain experience from the operation of an international monitoring system and to demonstrate achievable capabilities. Once the ongoing redesign and testing of the system are concluded, this could be an interesting possibility.

Verification Arrangements within the Nuclear-Weapon States

In addition to the establishment of a global seismological monitoring system, the possibility has been discussed of implementing additional verification measures in the nuclear weapon States, especially in the United States and the USSR. These measures are aimed at improving the verification capability, primarily in selected critical areas such as test sites or areas containing cavities or low coupling ground *matériel* where the seismic signals from explosions will be substantially reduced. They could be designed in such a way as to enhance confidence by reducing the risk of generating false alarms through misinterpreting local earthquakes or large chemical explosions.

At the summit meeting of the Six-Nation Initiative in Mexico in August 1986 a document on verification was presented as an annex to the Mexico Declaration. This document on verification contains an offer by the six States to assist in the monitoring of the cessation of nuclear testing by the United States and the USSR.

Three specific verification arrangements were offered to facilitate a mutually agreed moratorium. They are in principle also applicable to other political frameworks. They are as follows:

1. To establish and operate seismological recording stations at or close to the established test sites in the two countries, i.e., Nevada in the United States and Semipalatinsk and Novaya Zemlya in the USSR. By operating stations in the distance range of up to 100–200 km from the source region, weak explosions down to and even below 1 ton can be detected. The existing test sites, where facilities for nuclear testing are well developed and where considerable experience has been accumulated, can thus be monitored with confidence.

2. To "internationalize" a number—tentatively 25-30—of the existing seismological stations in the United States and the USSR by placing observers from the six countries at those stations. The purpose of the observers is to certify the authenticity of data provided by these "in-country stations." These seismological stations were originally established to study earthquakes, and their data should also be used primarily to monitor earthquakes, which frequently occur in the two countries. To provide an adequate monitoring of earthquakes, and thereby reduce the risk of their being misinterpreted as clandestine explosions, is an essential element of a verification system. Local stations will, among other things, provide data for accurate depth estimation. The human observers should subsequently be replaced by automatic data-authentication devices.

3. To conduct on-site inspections of large chemical explosions to confirm that the explosions are non-nuclear. As there is at present no way to differentiate between the seismic signals from chemical explosions and those from nuclear explosions, on-site inspections have to be used. Inspections should be conducted upon invitation and should cover not only the time of the explosion but also some time before and perhaps also some time after the explosion. The sponsors of the Six-Nation Initiative have offered to co-operate with the United States and the USSR in developing the necessary on-site inspection techniques and to conduct such inspections.

These temporary verification measures could be implemented on short notice so as not to delay the cessation of nuclear testing. The offers given in the annex to the Mexico Declaration were limited to a period of one year, the intention being that they should subsequently be replaced by permanent verification arrangements. As there has so far not been any agreement between the United States and the USSR on a moratorium or any other arrangement to halt nuclear testing, these verification arrangements have not yet been implemented.

In addition to the verification measures illustrated by the Mexico Declaration, it might be appropriate to discuss the establishment of monitoring devices at large standing cavities, created either by large nuclear explosions or through mining, to provide confidence that such cavities are not being used to conceal clandestine nuclear tests.

Verification of a Step-by-Step Approach to a Comprehensive Test-Ban Treaty

The United States and the USSR now seem to be engaged in some kind of step-by-step reduction of their nuclear testing. It is to be hoped that the arrangements will be such as to effectively limit the possibility of weapons development. In any case, many countries, including Sweden, would be critical of a step-by-step approach if it would not explicitly lead to a comprehensive test-ban treaty within a defined period of time.

The step-by-step process began in fact in 1974 with the conclusion of the 150-kiloton threshold test-ban Treaty. Such a process is likely to include both a successive lowering of the maximum yield of the explosions, for example the threshold, and a limitation on the number of tests to be conducted. The tests would probably have to be restricted to one test site in each country and a comprehensive test ban should in fact be established outside these test areas. There might be various scenarios as regards the ways to lower the yield threshold and to limit the number of tests.

The monitoring of a step-by-step approach involves two basic considerations:

1. Monitoring defined test areas to count the number of explosions and to establish that the yields of these explosions do not exceed the agreed threshold;
2. Monitoring the territories of the United States and the USSR to provide confidence that no explosions are conducted outside the test areas and that no earthquake is misinterpreted as a clandestine test.

The test sites can, as has been described earlier, be monitored by close-in stations which will also provide fairly accurate yield estimates if calibration explosions are available in the actual test area. Bilateral United States-USSR calibration experiments are to be conducted at the Semipalatinsk and Nevada test sites involving on-site measurement, using the widely discussed CORRTEX[1] method.

To monitor the territories of the United States and the Soviet Union outside the test sites, a global seismic monitoring system as well as stations inside the two countries could be used, as discussed above.

Countries around the world have repeatedly expressed their readiness to assist in providing adequate verification of a comprehensive test-ban treaty, through an international verification system as well as through verification measures within the United States and the USSR. Given the political will of all countries, such verification measures could also be utilized for the multilateral verification of a step-by-step approach to a comprehensive test-ban treaty.

Note

1. Continuous Reflectometry for Radius vs. Time Experiments. The yield is determined from the speed of the shock wave close to the explosion point, measured by a down-hole cable.

AIR MONITORING AS A MEANS FOR VERIFICATION OF CHEMICAL DISARMAMENT

Jorma K. Miettinen*

Remote Air Monitoring

Since 1973 the Finnish Research Project on the Verification of Chemical Disarmament has been developing analytical techniques for use in the various tasks required by the convention on chemical disarmament which is being negotiated at the Conference on Disarmament (see Fig. 1).

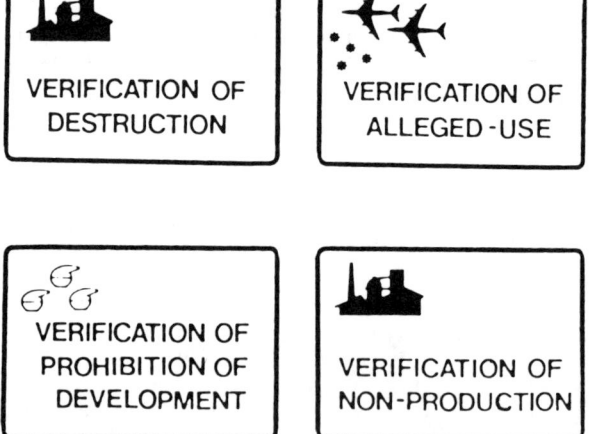

Figure 1. Verification tasks requiring chemical expertise

---

*Jorma K. Miettinen, Director of the Finnish Research Project on the Verification of Chemical Disarmament, is professor at the University of Helsinki, Finland. This contribution includes excerpts from a publication prepared for the government of Finland to present to the Conference on Disarmament.

During the first 10 years of the project, the spectra and other analytical data of some 60 organophosphorus compounds with nerve-agent potential, 60 of their degradation products, and 25 nonphosphorus warfare agents were published. The analytical techniques were summarized and their application evaluated in our report A.2, of 1984.

It has now been preliminarily agreed upon at the Conference on Disarmament that, under the proposed convention, a consultative committee should be established to oversee its implementation. Under it, an executive council will organize the arrangements for verification of compliance with the treaty and will direct the work of an inspectorate.

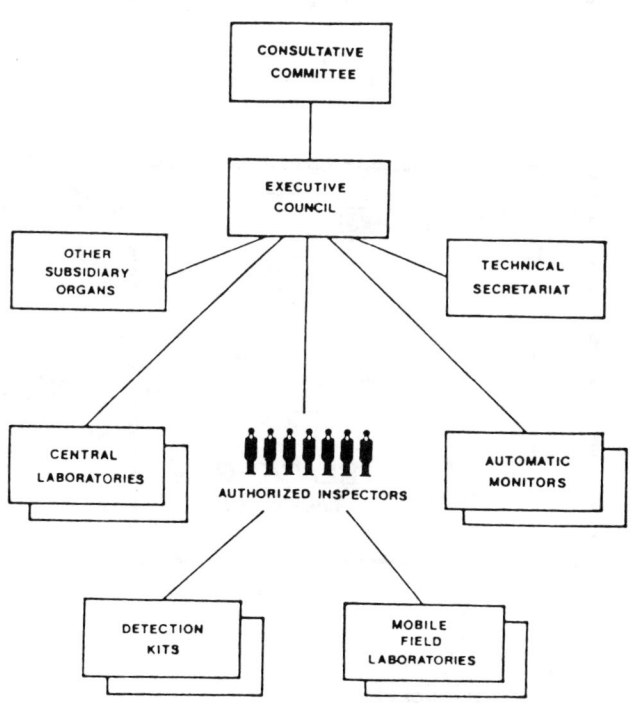

Figure 2. An approach to the gathering of information for the verification of chemical warfare agents.

Figure 2 shows in schematic form how we believe the technical aspects of verification could fit into the comprehensive verification system.

In support of authorized inspectors and sample analysis, we envisage a system of automatic black-box monitoring (Fig. 3). Wisely applied, this could save manpower, increase reliability, reduce intrusiveness and cost, and deliver real-time results. The applicability has been discussed in the "Proceedings of the Workshop on Automatic Monitoring of Verification of Chemical Disarmament."[1]

Until 1984 the goal of the project was to exploit the most promising modern techniques for the systematic collection of data for the identification of chemical warfare agents. In report C.2, of 1985, a new objective was chosen: to carry out concrete verification tasks in the field. We also wished to explore the functioning of a comprehensive verification system in practice. "Air Monitoring as a Means for the Verification of Chemical Disarmament" was taken as the first new area for investigation. A particular effort was made to develop sample collection methods and enlist the

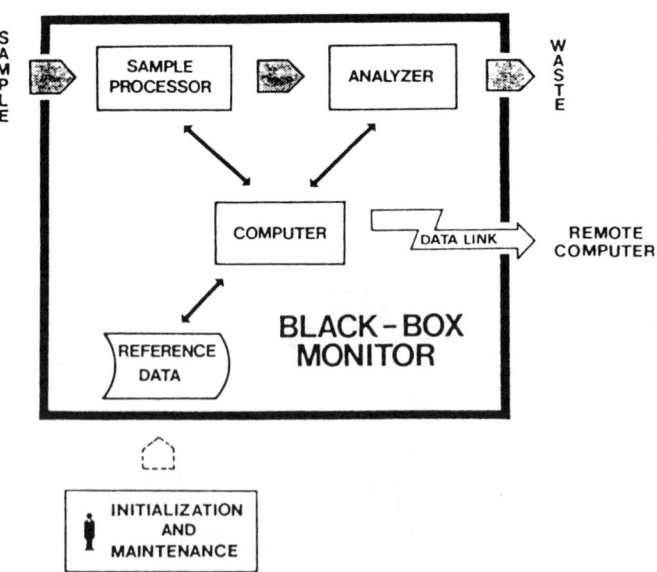

Figure 3. Schematic presentation of a black-box monitor.

support of meteorological expertise towards the eventual design of monitoring networks. Special attention was devoted to the development of methods for remote air monitoring.

The air matrix offers several advantages. First of all, air is a good sampling matrix because agents are likely to be released into the atmosphere from all kinds of activities to be controlled under the convention. Since the bulk of the air, that is, the permanent gases, need not be collected but passed through the sampler, traces of agents can be absorbed from large volumes of air onto a small volume of a suitable resin.

Secondly, analytical methods with sufficient sensitivity to allow identification of trace amounts of agents in a high background air matrix are already in existence. The knowledge that accidental release of one or two kilograms of an agent can be detected in another country, many hundreds of kilometers downwind, will surely have a deterrent effect on clandestine activities prohibited under the convention.

Thirdly, the same methods as the one being developed for the remote air analysis of chemical warfare agents can be applied to the analysis of industrial and urban pollutants. This dual applicability of the methods offers the great advantage that support for their development can then be obtained from several sources, and the station network that is likely to be erected in the future can serve both purposes.

Still remote air monitoring is a new and complex field. The thousands of compounds present in the ambient air will require highly selective identification methods. The problems in regard to automation of sample collection, concentration, analysis, data handling, and transfer have not yet been sold, although it is now known that they can be solved.

Our report C.2 of 1985 described in a general way the atmospheric dispersion of releases, the calculation of trajectories, the chemical reactions in the atmosphere causing transformation of chemical warfare agents, the composition of common air impurities, and the evaluation of sampling techniques. It described in detail the new method of high-volume air sampling and preparation of high-volume samples for analysis. A new mode of gas chromatography called retention spectrometry was also described.

In report C.3 of 1986 results of our first three field experiments were described. With the aid of the Finnish army and air force, three large-scale field experiments were carried out in which a mixture of three non-toxic simulants of warfare agents was dispersed as a fine aerosol on a hill with two smoke generators. Air-collection stations at distances from 5 to 140 km downwind were used and three sizes of collectors were applied:

low-volume (0.1 m³, medium-volume (1 m³) and high-volume (1000 m³). All three simulants could be detected at all distances.

This report, our third on air monitoring, covers the work done in the autumn of 1986. In order to gain more experience from the performance of the methods in the field, new field experiments, again conducted jointly with the army and air force, were carried out in the autumn of 1986.

This time we tested the release of aerosols at heights of 100 and 200 m, from an aircraft. Samples were collected by the three kinds of samplers described above at distances of up to 200 km downwind. Forecast of trajectories was indispensable for correct location of the sampling stations. Even at 200 km, all three simulants were detected. The aircraft sampling yielded the largest amounts of the simulants per sample, proving thereby to be the most effective collection technique.

A new type of field laboratory was developed, one in which the equipment is packed in containers, and from this, valuable information was collected. The laboratory is more convenient for transport over long distances, overseas for instance, than one built into a trailer. The containerized laboratory can be set up quickly, in any building or even in a tent.

A new technique based on low-volume Tenax GC sampling, thermal desorption, and two-stage gas chromatography was tested in the field laboratory. This method is important because it can easily be automated. The reliability of the identification was enhanced by combining retention index monitoring with retention spectrometry. This new instrumentation was used for the analysis of samples collected during a field experiment carried out for the purpose of evaluating the feasibility of delayed verification after "alleged use" of nerve agents. The instrumentation worked well, leading us to propose it for continuous ambient air monitoring at manned meteorological stations.

The field experiments confirmed that the systems developed do indeed work in the field, at least under reasonable weather conditions. Much valuable experience on the use of different sample collection and analytical techniques was gathered.

Skill in meteorological trajectory calculation and understanding of the meteorological behavior of aerosol clouds are prerequisites of remote air monitoring. This is a difficult area, and not within the scope of this project. While our tests contributed little to the body of meteorological knowledge, meteorological models allowed trajectories to be forecast well enough for us to obtain large enough samples for analysis at almost all distances up to 200 km.

In the near future, the new techniques of meteorological observation should permit greatly improved accuracy of analysis and forecasting. The possibility of tracking a specific air mass will then improve radically. On the basis of the meteorological analyses that are now technically feasible and of the results of our field tests, we believe that long-range detection of agents should be possible with a network of stations spaced about 400 to 500 km apart.

Development of remote air monitoring into a reliable verification technique will require extensive international collaboration in the development of methods and in the sharing of information on observed or suspected releases and on the movement of agent clouds. There is, however, good reason to believe that remote air monitoring will soon be developed, if not for chemical disarmament verification, then for control of civilian air pollution. We hope that the two can be developed together since this will hasten the progress and be cost-effective.

Basic Requirements of an Air-Monitoring System of Compliance Verification

Among the negotiators for a comprehensive ban on chemical weapons, there seems to be agreement that the proposed treaty must be provided with an effective verification system. Verification will rely on systematic national and international inspections, challenge inspections, and instrumental monitoring of declared stockpiles of chemical munitions, destruction plants, closed production plants, single small-scale facilities, and the civilian chemical industry. But how can the undeclared activities be detected?

In report C.2 we suggested that permanent air monitoring stations could be established for continuous monitoring. The stations could be either fully automatic stand-alone systems or else integrated into the monitoring schemes of existing environmental laboratories.

A fully automatic continuous air monitoring system requires an easy and reliable sampling technique in addition to the instrumentation carrying out automatic analysis. Low-volume sampling based on Tenax GC resin as the adsorbent proved to be reliable and quantitative for all chemical warfare agents tested in this study except for VX, which was irreversibly adsorbed in the sampling system. The agents can be recovered almost quantitatively (95 percent) in 30-dm³ air samples at pg-level. Before adoption of the sampling system, the safe sampling volumes at ambient temperature must be established.

We tested instrumentation for monitoring stations, based on gas chromatography, which is sensitive, reliable and low-cost, though not yet fully automatic. The instrumentation exploits low-volume Tenax GC sampling, thermal desorption, 2-stage gas chromatography for separation of overlapping peaks, and identification by retention index monitoring in combination with retention spectrometry. No major problems are envisaged in the development of a fully automatic system. The instrumentation is easily transportable in containers and could be used as part of the analytical equipment of an international inspection team during on-site visits.

At the present state of the art, high-volume air samples must be manually prepared, and analysed with sophisticated analytical instruments. Several sensitive and reliable techniques are available for the identification of agents in high background samples. The potential of MS/MS was already demonstrated in our earlier reports C.2 of 1985, and C.3 of 1986. Fourier transform infrared spectrometry becomes much more valuable when used on-line with gas chromatography. If 2-stage gas chromatography were used instead of conventional GC for sample introduction, the spectra of pure compounds could be recorded even from high background matrices. When the matrix isolation technique is available as well, the sensitivity of the method becomes comparable to that of mass spectrometry.

The sensitivity of high field (400 MHz) nuclear magnetic resonance spectrometry is not yet competitive with the two spectrometric techniques just mentioned. The selectivity of ^{31}P and ^{19}F NMR may nevertheless find a place for NMR in the identification of unknown compounds in concentrated air samples. If the toxic compounds in air samples can be located, the sensitivity of the spectrometric techniques (MS/MS, GC-FTIR, and ^{31}P and ^{19}F NMR) may be sufficient to allow structural elucidation.

The usefulness of retention spectrometry for the identification of known compounds in complex background matrices is now well established, and the selectivity and sensitivity of the enzymatic method make it highly competitive even for quantitative analyses of nerve agents in air samples. The use of a diode array detector in conjunction with retention index monitoring increases the reliability of the identification of model agents in high performance liquid chromatographic analysis.

A global network consisting of automatic air monitoring stations, 400–

500 km apart, and selected stations capable of collecting and analyzing high-volume samples would seem both adequate and realistic. Present developments in meteorological observation technology will improve radically the possibility of tracking specific air masses and these can probably be developed into routine operations within a few years, that is, they could be operative when the proposed convention enters into force. If monitoring stations were spaced 400 to 500 km apart, chemical warfare agents could be detected before major atmospheric transformation.

Should the monitors detect banned agents in the air, the possible emission site could be determined by meteorological calculations similar to those done when a rise in the level of background radioactivity is detected. Aircraft could be dispatched to collect large air samples from the designated air mass if further confirmation of the results was considered necessary.

A field test designed to evaluate the delayed verification of chemical warfare agents showed that sarin could be unambiguously identified from air samples collected almost two weeks after the contamination of soil. As sarin is one of the most volatile agents, detection of chemical warfare agents at air monitoring stations might reasonably be confirmed by collecting air samples at the suspect emission site even a few weeks later.

Field tests demonstrated the feasibility of monitoring production processes outside the production premises. At least chemicals having considerable vapour pressure can be detected by near-site air monitoring. Near-site monitoring may nevertheless be difficult where a hermetic production facility incinerates all exhaust gases and water before release. We do not yet know the feasibility of detecting hidden stockpiles by collecting air samples outside the stockpile premises. On the other hand, air samples may be very informative when collected during on-site inspections inside the facilities and stockpiles.

Note

1. Proceedings of the Workshop on Automatic Monitoring in the Verification of Chemical Disarmament, 12–14 February 1987, held in Helsinki, Finland.

CLOSING REMARKS

Yasushi Akashi[*]

We have had a full week, dealing with a very complex issue. I have been impressed by the constructive atmosphere that has prevailed, and I wish to express my sincere thanks to all of you for your valuable remarks and co-operation. You have made my task as Chairman very easy.

As I said at the beginning of the week, we do not expect to go away with all the answers, but if we can facilitate free-ranging discussion and encourage a better mutual understanding of these sensitive political and technical issues, then we in the Department for Disarmament Affairs of the United Nations believe that we shall have achieved our purpose. It is my opinion—and I hope it is yours—that we have indeed achieved that purpose.

I have been struck by the harmony of view of many of the papers and statements. Several participants have commented on the similarity of some of the themes and I believe this augurs well for the future.

During the week we have explored many aspects of multilateral verification. We are all more aware now of some of the difficulties that will arise, and of some of the questions for which answers will have to be found. At the same time, there has been broad recognition of the fact that multilateral arms control and disarmament agreements will demand some form of multilateral verification, for which appropriate machinery and institutional arrangements will have to be made.

We have also heard some differing opinions with regard to the way in which this might be achieved. Some have felt that verification arrangements are treaty-specific, requiring dedicated arrangements; others have felt that an international verification organization will be needed, which would be less costly than separate operations and at the same time more efficient in the use of expertise and administrative backing.

I believe there was a slight convergence of views towards acceptance of some common services, to provide administrative support and training, which may be required after several treaties have been concluded and verification mechanisms put in place. Although inspectors for specific treaties have to have special backgrounds, in order to avoid a certain amount

---

[*]Undersecretary General for Disarmament Affairs

of duplication which could arise, and to make use of accumulated experience and skills, gradually we might find a certain type of co-ordination, if not unification. Perhaps, after several treaties, there might be some kind of federated or confederated approach in which certain functions could be done centrally and other functions would remain specific. I am just projecting the possibility of an evolution of institutional trends.

We have been given valuable information on the practice and experience of the International Atomic Energy Agency and on the sort of down-to-earth, practical problems that will have to be resolved. With a chemical weapons convention not far off, we hope, some of these problems are already almost upon us and we have no time to waste. The principles of verification developed in the United Nations Disarmament Commission seem to have gained wide acceptance at this meeting, although one or two changes were suggested. I am very glad that this year's Chairman of the UNDC, Ambassador Davidson Hepburn, has been with us and I hope the experience of this week will be of help to him in the Commission's consideration of the issue.

Oddly enough, however, there seems as yet to be no clear definition or understanding of the term "verification" in the context of disarmament, and this is one of the issues that needs further study.

Several participants have referred to methods of verification, ranging from national technical means to on-site challenge inspections. Clearly, some methods used in bilateral verification will be applicable to multilateral verification arrangements, and some will not. The importance of the timely exchange of data and information and the need for openness and transparency were highlighted, as was the need to protect the interests of national security and commercial confidentiality. At the same time, the development of confidence and trust is essential.

I believe we have had a very useful exchange of views on the question whether or not a technological gap is opening between weapons and verification capabilities. The presence among us of a number of technical and scientific experts has been of great help to us in that part of our discussion. At the same time, however, it has been pointed out that verification is not just a technical matter, and that part of the gap can and must be bridged by the adoption of appropriate inspection procedures. This points toward a need for an approach involving more interaction between politics and science in the future.

I am sure that the exposure of the group to the scientific knowledge and experience presented on current techniques and arrangements for verification and on the seismological measurement of underground nuclear explosions as well as chemical weapons measurements has been most useful.

Finally, where do we go from here? A major conclusion is obvious—namely, that we are only at the beginning of a long road. It seems to me that it would be valuable if the Disarmament Commission could conclude its discussion of this first stage with some form of acceptance of general principles. Clearly, the topic of multilateral verification and a possible role for the United Nations in some form will be raised at the forthcoming special session of the General Assembly in June, when the Six Nations present their initiative. Later in the year, it seems likely that the subject of multilateral verification will be taken up at the regular session of the General Assembly, and we have already heard the thought expressed that there is much that needs study by a group of governmental experts. In this important disarmament matter, I and my Department stand ready to offer every assistance.

It remains now for me to conclude my remarks by thanking all of you for coming so far and making such thoughtful and positive contributions to this week's discussions. I wish to express our deep appreciation to our Soviet hosts for their warm and generous hospitality here in Sochi, and for their contribution to the World Disarmament Campaign that has made it possible. The tireless efforts and dedication of the members of the Soviet Peace Committee, the interpreters, and all who have contributed to make this week so worth while and enjoyable have our highest praise.

List of Participants & Observers

Prof. Tunde Adeniran, Department of Political Science, University of Ibadan, Nigeria

Ambassador Aleksandr A. Bessmertnykh, Deputy Minister of Foreign Affairs, USSR

Mr. Genrikh Borovik, President, Soviet Peace Committee, USSR

Mr. Ludger Buerstedde, Chief, Division for Security, Disarmament and Arms Control in Europe, Ministry of Foreign Affairs, Federal Republic of Germany

Ambassador Julio César Carasales, Special Advisor to Secretary of State for International Relations, Disarmament Department, Ministry of Foreign Affairs, Argentina

Mr. Glenn R. Cella, Senior Fellow, Center for the Study of Foreign Affairs, U.S.A.

Colonel General N. F. Chervov, Chief, Department of Treaties and Legal Affairs, Armed Forces of the USSR, USSR

Ambassadeur de France Gilles Curien, Ministry of Foreign Affairs, France

Mr. Ian Cuthbertson, Resident Fellow, Institute for East-West Security Studies, United Kingdom

Mr. Michael J. Dawson, First Secretary, Embassy of Canada at Moscow

Dr. James E. Dougherty, Professor of Politics, St. Joseph's University, U.S.A.

Admiral Sir James Eberle, GCB, Director, Royal Institute of International Affairs, United Kingdom

Ambassador Fan Guoxiang, Ambassador of the People's Republic of China to the Conference on Disarmament

Lieutenant General Daniel O. Graham, Director, High Frontier Organization, U.S.A.

Mr. Claude Heller, Director General for the United Nations, Ministry of Foreign Affairs, Mexico

Ambassador Ryukichi Imai, Former Ambassador to the Conference on Disarmament, Japan

Brigadier Anatoly Kamazima, Ministry of Defence and National Service, Tanzania

Ambassador Abdelmajid Karoui, Permanent Mission of Tunisia to the United Nations

Prof. Dr. Peter Klein, Deputy Director, Institute of International Policy and Economics, German Democratic Republic

Ambassador Dimiter Kostov, Director, United Nations and Disarmament Affairs Department, Ministry of Foreign Affairs, Bulgaria

Ambassador Jorge Morelli-Pando, Embassy of Peru at Vienna

Lieutenant Colonel W. Alexander Morrison, Counsellor, Permanent Mission of Canada to the United Nations

Prof. Dr. hab. Wojciech Multan, Deputy Director, Polish Institute for International Affairs, Poland

Mr. John Cameron Okely, Counsellor, Permanent Mission of Australia to the United Nations

Dr. Torleiv Orhaug, Director of Technology, National Defence Research Institute, Sweden

Mr. Frantisek Penazka, Head of Department of International Organizations, Ministry of Foreign Affairs, Czechoslovakia

Dr. Sigrid Pöllinger, Professor, University Centre for Peace Research, Austria

Mr. Mohamed Rahhali, Head of Division of the United Nations, Ministry of Foreign Affairs and Co-operation, Morocco

Ambassador Maharajakrishna Rasgotra, Former Foreign Secretary, India

Ambassador Edward Rowny, Special Advisor to the President and Secretary of State for Arms Control Matters, U.S.A.

Ambassador Tony K. Siddique, Embassy of Singapore at Bonn

Mr. Tibor Toth, Deputy Head, Department of International Organizations, Ministry of Foreign Affairs, Hungary

Mr. Alexey A. Vasiliev, Head of Division for Outer Space, Institute of USA and Canada Studies, Academy of Sciences, USSR

PART TWO

Participants

Ambassador Robert Barker, Assistant to Secretary of Defense, U.S.A.

Mr. Adolf von Baeckmann, Adviser, Office of the Deputy Director-General, International Atomic Energy Agency, Austria

Mr. Peter W. Basham, Chief, Seismology Program, Geological Survey of Canada, Canada

Major General Guely V. Batenin, Military Expert, Central Committee of the Communist Party, USSR

Ambassador Jaroslaw Cesar, Chief of the International Organizations Department, Ministry of Foreign Affairs, Czechoslovakia

Mr. F. Ronald Cleminson, Head of Verification Research Unit, Department of External Affairs, Canada

The Honorable William A. Cockell, Jr., Deputy Assistant to the President for National Security Affairs, U.S.A.

Dr. Ola Dahlman, Director, Swedish National Defence Research Institute, Sweden

Mr. Jean Desazars de Montgailhard, Deputy-Director for Disarmament, Ministry of Foreign Affairs, France

Major General Dr. Esmat Z. Ezz, Egyptian Armed Forces, Egypt

Mr. Wilhelm Nikolai Germann, Member of the Delegation of the Federal Republic of Germany to the Conference on Disarmament

Ambassador Chinmaya Rajaninath Gharekhan, Permanent Representative of India to the United Nations

Prof. Mikhail V. Gochberg, Deputy Director, Institute of Earth Physics, Academy of Sciences, USSR

Colonel General Oleg A. Grinevsky, Ambassador-at-Large, Ministry of Foreign Affairs, USSR

Ambassador Lynn M. Hansen, Assistant Director, Arms Control and Disarmament Agency, U.S.A.

Ambassador Davidson L. Hepburn, Permanent Representative of the Bahamas to the United Nations

Ambassador Victor L. Issraelyan, Professor, Diplomatic Academy of the Ministry of Foreign Affairs, USSR

Ambassador Borislav Konstantinov, Ministry of Foreign Affairs, Bulgaria

Mr. Michael Krepon, Director, Verification Project, Carnegie Endowment, U.S.A.

Prof. Jorma K. Miettinen, University of Helsinki, Finland

Mr. Oleg F. Nemets, Academician, Nuclear Research Institute, Academy of Sciences, USSR

Dr. Arie J. J. Ooms, Director, Prins Maurits Laboratory, The Netherlands

Mr. Zhuang Qubing, Research Fellow, Institute of International Studies, People's Republic of China

Dr. Frode Ringdal, Director, Norwegian Seismic Array, Norway

Mr. Mohamed Abdelhalim Said, Ministry of Foreign Affairs, Egypt

Mr. Benjamin Sanders, Head, Programme for Promoting Nuclear Non-Proliferation (New York)

Ambassador Robert J. van Schaik, Permanent Representative of the Kingdom of the Netherlands to the United Nations Office at Geneva

Ambassador Tessa A. H. Solesby, Representative of the United Kingdom of Great Britain and Northern Ireland to the Conference on Disarmament

Mr. Serge Sur, Deputy Director, United Nations Institute for Disarmament Research (Geneva)

Ambassador Adolfo Raul Taylhardat, Permanent Representative of Venezuela to the United Nations Office at Geneva

Dr. Hubert Thielicke, Head of Section, Division for United Nations Affairs, Ministry for Foreign Affairs (Berlin)

Mr. Kazimierz Tomaszewski, Counsellor, Permanent Mission of the Polish People's Republic to the United Nations

Mr. Franklin E. Walker, Senior Scientist, Lawrence Livermore National Laboratory, U.S.A.

Mr. Ronald Walker, First Assistant Secretary, Disarmament Defense and Nuclear Division, Department of Foreign Affairs and Trade, Australia

Ambassador Chusei Yamada, Representative of Japan to the Conference on Disarmament

Observers

Mr. I. Filin, Secretary, Soviet Peace Committee, USSR

Mr. O. M. Lisov, Captain First Class, Ministry of Defence, USSR

Mr. V. G. Martynov, Senior Research Fellow, Institute of Earth Physics, Academy of Sciences, USSR

Mr. O. Mitrenko, Executive Council, Krasnodar Region, USSR

Ms. Cisca Spencer, Embassy of Australia at Moscow

Mr. Jun Yamada, Embassy of Japan at Moscow